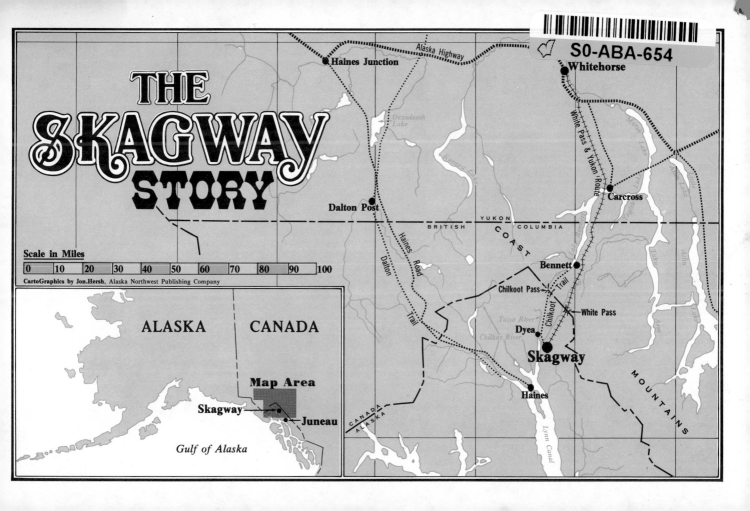

THE SKAGWAY STORY

Scale in Miles

0 10 20 30 40 50 60 70 80 90 100

CartoGraphics by Jon.Hersh, Alaska Northwest Publishing Company

ALASKA   CANADA

Map Area

Skagway

Juneau

Gulf of Alaska

Haines Junction

Alaska Highway

Whitehorse

Dezadeash Lake

Dalton Post

White Pass & Yukon Route

Carcross

YUKON

BRITISH   COLUMBIA

COAST

Haines Road

Dalton Trail

Bennett

Chilkoot Pass

Chilkoot Trail

White Pass

Taiya River

Dyea

Chilkat River

Skagway

Haines

MOUNTAINS

CANADA
ALASKA

Lynn Canal

THE SKAGWAY STORY

A history of Alaska's most famous gold rush town
and of some of the
people who made that history.

HOWARD CLIFFORD

ALASKA NORTHWEST PUBLISHING COMPANY
Anchorage, Alaska

First Printing 1975
Third Printing 1978

Library of Congress Cataloging in Publication Data:
Clifford Howard.
    The Skagway Story.
    Bibliography: p.
    1. Skagway, Alaska — History.   2. Skagway, Alaska — Gold discoveries. 3. Skagway, Alaska — Biography. I. Title.
F914.S7C47   979.8'2   75-13918   ISBN 0-88240-046-0

Edited by Byron Fish
Layout and design by Roz Pape

Alaska Northwest Publishing Company
Box 4-EEE, Anchorage, Alaska 99509

Printed in U.S.A.

Title page—*The* Queen *as she loaded for Skagway on the Seattle waterfront.*

TABLE OF CONTENTS

FOREWORD

We've always had a keen interest in the details of Skagway's past as a rip-roaring gold rush town, and we've spent many years gathering little-known facts, recollections of pioneers who were there, memorabilia, photographs from dusty trunks in attics and basements . . . with the hope that we could one day share *The Skagway Story* with others who love the Northland and appreciate its past.

This book is a link connecting the Skagway of yesteryear—the Skagway of Capt. Billy Moore, Jefferson Randolph "Soapy" Smith, Frank Reid, the vigilantes and others—with the Skagway of today . . . still a vital transportation link for the mineral-rich Yukon.

Landmarks of the past are fading in Skagway. Hardly a year goes by without the collapse of one old building or another. Our hope is that *The Skagway Story*, in its way, will help keep alive the excitement of the little town on the shores of Lynn Canal . . . and entertain those who live there, or used to live there, or have recently "discovered" Skagway in their travels.

Our deepest thanks to the following for their help in assembling *The Skagway Story:*

Bobby Sheldon, who went to Skagway as a youngster and is one of the few remaining witnesses to the shootout between Soapy Smith and Frank Reid; Randolph J. Smith and Joseph J. Smith, grandsons of Soapy; Mary Kopanski, granddaughter of Harriet Pullen; Bob Monroe of the University of Washington Library; Bob De Armond, editor of *The ALASKA JOURNAL* (also published by Alaska Northwest Publishing Company); and the staff of Skagway's Golden North Hotel.

Also Frances Richter, Edna and George Rapuzzi, the Right Reverend G. Edgar Gallant, Georgette and Jack Kirmse, Cy Coyne, P. S. Ganty, Jack Conway, Sister Mary Luca, Barbara Kalen, Bill Feero, the late Mavis Soldin and many others.

Thank you!

—*Howard Clifford*
January 1975

Capt. William "Billy" Moore, founder of Skagway and discoverer of the route over the White Pass to the Yukon. Captain Moore played a prominent role in the early day development of Skagway and was one of the first to realize the importance of a railroad over White Pass.

William Ogilvie, Canadian government surveyor, hired Captain Moore to seek a better route over the mountains from tidewater at Skagway to the Yukon.

SKAGWAY'S FIRST SETTLER

The town variously known as Skagus, Mooresville, Skaguay and finally Skagway, the name it bears today, was first settled on October 20, 1887, by an old seafaring man, Capt. William "Billy" Moore, who had made and lost several fortunes as a sometimes riverboat captain and pilot, prospector, packer and trader.

Captain Moore staked his claim to 160 acres and pitched his tent on a small knoll alongside a creek to become the first settler, although Indians and others had visited the area previously to hunt and fish. That fall Captain Moore started construction of a pier on the shallow tide flats of Skagway Bay, not only to enable him and his son Ben to land equipment and supplies, but also because he decided that this location would be the most logical for a town to serve the route to the Yukon, which he believed was rich in minerals yet to be discovered.

Earlier in 1887 Captain Moore had contracted to go into the Yukon country with a Canadian government survey party headed by William Ogilvie. Moore was to provide the know-how of packing over wilderness trails, and build and navigate a barge with supplies down the Yukon River.

Entry into the upper Yukon Valley at that time was by way of the Chilkoot Trail, a precipitous and rugged route that taxed men's strength and courage to the utmost. The old man had heard there was another route into the upper Yukon, 600 feet less in altitude, that could be reached from Skagway Bay. He was determined to test the feasibility of the new route, so while the Ogilvie party took the old trail, Captain Moore started up the Skagway River. Accompanied by an Indian named Skookum Jim, who was later to be a co-discoverer of the Klondike gold field, he struggled up over a pass 45 miles long. There was no trail of any kind and traveling entailed perilous switchbacks over precipitous hillsides and canyons. It took the Moore party days to join Ogilvie at Lake Bennett, one of the headwaters of the Yukon. Captain Moore was enthusiastic about the new route he had discovered. Ogilvie named White Pass after Thomas White, Canadian Minister of the Interior.

As Ogilvie recalled later, the old man's imagination was inspired. "Every night during the two months he remained with us, he would picture the tons of yellow dust yet to be found in the Yukon Valley. He decided then and there that Skagway would be the entry point to the golden fields—and White Pass would reverberate with the rumble of railway trains carrying supplies."

Captain Moore's predictions proved amazingly accurate. In 1896 gold was discovered on the river the world came to know as the Klondike, triggering the greatest stampede in history.

The nearest inhabitants to Captain Moore's Skagway acreage were Indians at Smuggler's Cove, some miles away, and the Healy and Wilson Trading Post at Dyea founded in 1885-86 by John J. Healy. Haines Mission, 15 miles away, was the only other white settlement in the area.

Prospectors had begun their assault on the Yukon Valley during the 1870's. In 1873 Arthur Harper used the Peace and Mackenzie rivers to reach the Yukon.

2

Skookum Jim, an Indian guide, accompanied Captain Moore on his historic trip over the White Pass. Skookum Jim was later to be one of the co-discoverers of the Klondike gold fields.

The Healy and Wilson store at Dyea, operated by John J. Healy and Edgar Wilson, was the main supply post for those going over the Chilkoot Pass in the early days of the gold rush. The trading post was founded in 1885-86. This photo was taken on July 4, 1898, during the height of the rush to the Klondike.

VOGEE COLLECTION. YUKON ARCHIVES

George Holt in 1874 crossed directly into the valley via the Chilkoot Pass, sneaking past the Indians who controlled the route at the time. The first group to use the route was the Edmund Bean party of 20 men in 1880. The long Bering Sea-Yukon River route was used by Ed Schieffelin in 1882.

By 1886 some 200 miners had crossed over the Chilkoot Pass and reached the mouth of the Stewart River, where in a single year some $100,000 of fine placer gold was panned from the sand bars. In 1888 Captain Moore finished the log house started the previous fall and extended pilings for the pier farther into the water. Work also progressed during the summer months on the cabin site, and on the White Pass or Skagway Trail which Captain Moore was developing.

In 1895 the first group of miners, seven young men from California, made the trip over the Moore trail to the headwaters of the Yukon. The first woman to hike over the White Pass was Miss Jessie McDougall of Seattle. On that trip Miss McDougall had the misfortune to break her leg near White Horse Rapids, and her rescue in midwinter 1897-98 was one of the thrillers of the period. She returned to Seattle that same winter, recovered, and came back over the trail the next spring to continue her trip to the Klondike.

In 1896 Captain Moore secured a Dominion Government contract to deliver the Royal Mail from Juneau to Fortymile (misspelled Forty Mile on many occasions), the first such contract ever awarded for delivery of mail into the Yukon. Captain Moore was now 74 years of age, but still as tough and hardbitten as the country he had to challenge. With the assistance of his son Ben he fulfilled the mail contract—a remarkable feat of endurance.

For years Captain Moore had tried to win financial support for his Skagway venture from the business community in Victoria, but without success. Perhaps too many remembered his sorry financial history. In 1886 Captain Moore approached E. D. Billinghurst of the B.C. Development Co., Ltd., who was an agent for an English promoter and capitalist named C. H. Wilkinson. Captain Moore was able to arrange for an advance of $1,800 for supplies, 2 horses, a couple of cows and 6,000 board feet of lumber in return for a lien on his preemption at Skagway Bay. This enabled

Capt. William "Billy" Moore's original cabin, the first structure built in Skagway. Captain Moore was ousted from this cabin and the structure moved from its original site by Frank Reid and others who took over the area by force when they landed at Skagway en route to the gold rush. The cabin is now located on the Kirmse property in Skagway.

HOWARD CLIFFORD

5

Captain Moore's sawmill in operation on the flats of Skagway in the fall of 1897. The mill provided the lumber for the building of the town, seen in the background, and netted Captain Moore a small fortune.

UNIVERSITY OF WASHINGTON LIBRARY

him to start work on improving the wharf against the steep bank with good depth of water, as the agreement also guaranteed wages for five men for the season. Captain Moore also had an official survey made of his 160 acres by Charles Garside, deputy United States surveyor from Juneau.

Later 15 men were employed and Captain Moore improved the homestead, built a sawmill and procured a steam pile driver with which the wharf was extended into Skagway Bay. Work was started also on a pack trail along the bank of the Skagway River and canyons crossed with the necessary bridges.

Robert Henderson was one of the prospectors on a river the Natives called *Thron-Diuck*, meaning "Hammer-Water," so named because the Indians hammered stakes in the stream to build salmon traps. The Klondike (early spelling was Clondyke as the miners pronounced it) had six tributaries which later proved to be among the richest creeks in the world. Henderson found gold in 1896—8 cents worth per can—with promise of more. He mentioned his find to George Washington Carmack (Siwash George), a Californian who had reached the Yukon in the 1880's and who had married the daughter of a Tagish chief. Carmack, with his two brothers-in-law, Skookum Jim and Tagish Charlie, searched for colors along the waterways of the Yukon. On August 14, 1896, the three were working Rabbit Creek and found gold lying between the flakey slabs of rock, "like cheese in a sandwich." The next morning the trio staked their claim to history. Up and down the Yukon the news spread. By the end of August all of Bonanza Creek (as Rabbit Creek became known) had been staked. Claims changed hands rapidly. One man sold his claim for $800, to find in 3 years that it was worth $1 million. Gold-crazed men poured into the diggings as winter set in.

The outside world knew nothing of the gold discovery. At Fortymile, William Ogilvie was searching for some means to apprise his government in Ottawa of the situation.

Few elected to attempt the tortuous 700-mile journey up the river from the Canadian side to the Chilkoot Pass. Captain Moore, a remarkable, tough old man, had just completed his mail run from Juneau to Fortymile and Circle City and was heading back again when he agreed to take Ogilvie's brief message. During the trip he overtook a U.S. mail carrier who had abandoned his sled because his dogs had given out, and an Indian was hauling the mail sack. A few days later he overtook a party which had left a day ahead of him. Still later he caught up with another group that had left 10 days prior to his departure with express and Canadian government dispatches, and who had only 2 days' provisions to last them 220 miles. He rendered assistance and enabled the group to reach the coast. Without his help they would have faced starvation.

Ogilvie's preliminary report on the Klondike was sent to Ottawa, where nobody paid any attention to it. In January Ogilvie tried again. Once more the message received the same reception in Ottawa— although eventually an austere little pamphlet was published, to create not a ripple of interest.

Such, however, was not the case when on July 15, 1897, the *SS Excelsior* steamed into San Francisco laden with a score or so of prospectors and hundreds of thousands of dollars worth of gold, followed a couple of days later by the *SS Portland*, which docked in

Seattle with its famed "ton of gold." The country, in the midst of a depression, went gold happy—especially Seattle and San Francisco. The Klondike gold rush was on.

Within 10 days after the arrival of the *Portland*, the cities of Seattle, Tacoma, Portland, San Francisco and Victoria were besieged by gold-hungry hordes headed North. The *Excelsior* headed North on her return voyage from San Francisco with a full load. The ticket agent could have sold ten times the space. One man struck it rich without going North. He bought a ticket and immediately sold it for $1,500—ten times its cost. Anything that could float was pressed into service.

THE RUSH BEGINS

Old Captain Moore thought he was ready for the rush that was to follow, but suddenly on July 29, 1897, his monarchy came to an end as the first gold rush ship, the Mail Steamer *Queen*, dumped its cargo of humanity at Skagway.

A committee representing some 200 of the advance guard of argonauts en route to the new gold fields came ashore, asked a few questions regarding routes, and sought permission to land on Captain Moore's property. Returning to the steamer, the advance guard decided that, on account of the large number of boats which would soon be flocking in, it would be good business to jump Captain Moore's claim. They would establish a city to take care of thousands of prospectors and feather their own nests in the process.

Captain Moore was unable to stop them. A town consisting of 3,600, 50- by 100-foot lots and 60-foot streets was laid out by one of the early arrivals, Frank H. Reid, a former county official from the Puget Sound country who came to Alaska after a brief stay in the Oregon Territory. Reid had been charged with killing a man in Sweet Home, Oregon, in 1879, but was acquitted on the basis of self-defense although the man killed was unarmed at the time.

The lots were quickly sold at good prices, but as they were soon all gone, the claim-jumpers worked out a new plan to resell all lots whose owners had gone "inside," or who were not in actual possession. This led to strenuous times. A miner would buy a lot, build a cabin, put his possessions in it and go over the pass only to return a few months later and discover that his belongings had been thrown out into the street or were gone altogether, and someone else was in possession of his property.

Captain Moore fared little better. Because of Reid's survey, his cabin was deemed to be in the middle of the town's main street. He was offered a lot on which to place his cabin but refused it, only to have a group of men finally take away his cabin and dump it on the tide flats. Captain Moore knew he had lost the fight. He moved onto land later given him, which today

The Mail Steamer Queen was one of many to land hordes of gold seekers on the beaches and wharves at Skagway. The vessel brought the first load of passengers to land on Captain Moore's wharf on July 29, 1897. Many others followed.

The arrival on Christmas Day, 1898, of the D. H. Pingree sled-dog team (shown in front of the Brannick Hotel) from Dawson City was considered quite a feat in Skagway. In the background is the St. James Hotel, another of Skagway's better facilities of the day, and in the distance is the original Golden North Hotel. The photo was taken on Bond Street (now Fourth Avenue) between Runnalls (State Street) and Broadway.

UNIVERSITY OF WASHINGTON LIBRARY

includes that occupied by the Kirmse residence, the old Pullen House and the present-day city hall. He continued his fight, and after a 4-year battle in the courts, was awarded 25 percent of the assessed value of all the lots within the original townsite of Skagway.

In the meantime he sold his wharf to the White Pass & Yukon Route for a large sum, reported in one newspaper as $125,000 and $5,000 a year for 10 years.

The indestructible Capt. William Moore ended his days in Victoria, British Columbia, a fairly wealthy man, dying there March 29, 1909. Few of the argonauts who forced him from his cabin, divested him of his forest and marched across his front yard came out with any gold or fortune.

Thus, the town of Skagway was conceived in lawlessness and grew up in violence.

Stampeders landing at Skagway about August 1, 1897. The first adventurers had gone ashore a few days earlier, but other than Captain Moore's crude wharf there were no docking facilities at Skagway at the time. Most early arrivals used horses and wagons or small boats to get their goods ashore while others floated what they could to the beach.

WINTER & POND COLLECTION, LIBRARY OF CONGRESS

13

14

SOAPY SMITH COMES & GOES

The disorderly state of affairs in Skagway led to constant discord and fighting. The situation was not helped by the almost daily arrival of boatload after boatload of prospectors. Skagway was soon a conglomeration not only of men, but women and children. The early arrivals included a Mrs. Leonard who later moved to Fortymile, and a Mrs. Crawford with two boys and a girl. All were hurrying to reach the gold fields, caring little what methods they used to get there.

Many new arrivals, losing their money one way or another, were forced to stay behind, and being without funds, it was not long before the town was a

Portrait of Jefferson Randolph "Soapy" Smith taken at the height of his career.

den of vice and all manner of crimes were being committed.

Judge John U. Smith, the U.S. commissioner at the time, was more interested in making money himself than he was in maintaining law and order. Commissioner Smith owed his position to Senator George W. McBride of Oregon. He had been appointed on July 8, 1897, and was one of the early gold rush arrivals. When Skagway was laid out he had rushed over from Dyea to secure the position of town recorder, and immediately set up a fee of $5.00 for recording deeds, a figure deemed excessive in those days.

Investigation indicated that the commissioner also had the habit of pocketing many of the fees, without recording the deeds. When a Canadian miner was drowned in fording the Taiya River, Commissioner Smith held an inquest and took charge of the deceased's effects, along with $149.10 collected by the miners for the benefit of his widow. Smith charged $30 for holding the inquest and did not forward the collection to the widow until pressure was brought on him. Despite many similar instances, Smith, because of his political pull, was able to hold onto the post until May 1898, when he was succeeded by C. A. Sehlbrede, a distinguished-looking man with some knowledge of Alaskan affairs.

The whole area between Lynn Canal and the headwaters of the Yukon, including Dyea and the White Pass trails as well as Skagway, had but a single U.S. deputy marshal, a man named Taylor. He later was removed from office by Commissioner Sehlbrede, but not before outlaw rule took over in Skagway. The town was split into two factions: the "skinners" and the "skinned." The skinners, however, had the better organization and stuck together so that those who were defrauded were unable to obtain redress. It was to such an ideal setting that Jefferson Randolph Smith (no relation to Commissioner Smith) arrived.

Jeff Smith was born in 1860 to a prominent and highly respected Southern family that fell into hard times following the Civil War. He worked his way west where he became a cowpuncher and rode the historic Chisholm Trail, dealt with Indians and Indian fighters, and learned to hold his own against the many desperadoes who infested the frontier. From the hard life of the cowpoke he graduated to the easy money of marked cards, gambling tables and con games.

Better known as "Soapy," he began his career as a con man selling soap supposedly wrapped in $5 to $50 bills, for a dollar. Needless to say, none but his favored henchmen ever were successful in purchasing a bar of soap still containing a bill in its wrappings, so skillful was Soapy as a sleight-of-hand artist.

Soapy was one of the most colorful and adroit of confidence men, outlaws and crooks in American history. Adverse to violence of any sort, Soapy found everything about Skagway to his liking, and there was nothing to prevent his declaring himself leader of the rougher element, which he lost no time in doing.

Whereas up to this time Skagway had suffered from claim-jumpers, petty criminals and their ilk, it was now destined to experience all the vices known to mining camps of the time. Gambling houses, saloons and dance halls sprang to life all over town. Soapy had a small, modest saloon situated on Holly Street (Sixth Avenue) where the Bank of Alaska now stands. Able to take over control of the town without force, his word was law. Many prospectors were robbed or

swindled out of their money and valuables through tricks credited to Soapy Smith and his gang during the fall and winter of 1897 and the spring and early summer of 1898.

Soapy was a literate man with highly developed social instincts, however, and his policy was to leave the townspeople alone as long as they did not interfere with his actions.

At the height of his power in Skagway, the *Seattle Post-Intelligencer* said of Smith that "about three-fourths of the stories about Soapy have been fiction." The *New York World* correspondent wrote,

---

Opposite—*Soapy Smith and some of his close associates in his saloon in Skagway. From left are: Nate Pollock the bartender, John Bowers, John Clancy, Soapy, the Sheeney Kid and another follower known only as "Red." Behind Clancy and Smith is a small area for a card game. There is no evidence of a large amount of gambling equipment as is so often written about when referring to "Jeff Smiths Parlor."*

HOWARD CLIFFORD COLLECTION

"He's the most gracious, kindhearted man I've ever met. To know him is to like him."

One of Soapy's early day companions in Skagway was Wilson Mizner, later a successful Broadway playwright who for a time was married to "the second richest woman in the world," the widow of Charles T. Yerkes. During the Florida land boom of the 1920's, Mizner made good use of some of the con-man deceptions that he had learned from the master. Later he became a successful writer and film producer in California, and was one of the founders of the famed Brown Derby restaurant in Hollywood.

Following the organization of the Skagway Guards, which Smith outfitted and offered in the service of his country in its war with Spain, and the famed Fourth of July parade, at which Smith was one of the parade marshals and was honored and praised by Alaska Governor John G. Brady for his civic interests, Soapy's career came to a quick and tragic end.

Merchants had begun to realize that lawlessness and disorder were rampant in Skagway and the big money they had visions of making for themselves was slipping through their fingers. A diminishing number

18

The unkept grave of Jefferson Randolph "Soapy" Smith, who died in the fatal gun duel with Frank Reid, is adjacent to Skagway's pioneer cemetery.

HOWARD CLIFFORD

The vigilante meeting which led to Soapy Smith's shootout with Frank Reid was held on Juneau wharf, center left. Soapy was shot at the entrance to the causeway of the wharf when he attempted to join the meeting. The wharf is located at the foot of Runnalls, now known as State Street. The wharf in the near foreground is Moore wharf, built by Capt. Billy Moore. It is still in use today as the docking area for cruise ships.

of transients were coming through Skagway as a result of the crime.

On July 7, 1898, a simple-appearing miner from the Yukon, John Douglas Stewart, came to town with his poke of some $2,700 in gold, and according to reports, "lost it." Some say he was robbed. Others say he lost it gambling in a local bar. A published interview with family members in Nanaimo, British Columbia, has it that he checked the poke in a hotel safe for the night, on the advice of two strangers with whom he chatted during the evening hours. The next morning when he went to claim his gold at the hotel desk, he was told there was nothing there and that "no one here has ever seen you before."

Whatever the story, Stewart immediately raised such a furor in town that the vigilante committee, long inactive, was reactivated and a meeting called. Demands were made by the committee that Smith

Portrait of Frank Reid.

bring about the return of the poke, although there was no proof that he had anything to do with its disappearance. Naturally Smith refused.

Thomas Whitten, of the Golden North Hotel, took over as chairman of the meeting of the Committee of One Hundred and One (as the vigilantes were known) when Samuel Graves, president of the White Pass & Yukon Route and newly elected permanent chairman of the group, would not call a meeting until a deadline established for the return of the Stewart gold had passed. The group met first in Sylvester Hall and then moved to the Juneau wharf. Whitten named Frank Reid, Capt. J. M. Tanner, Jesse Murphy and John Landers to guard the dock approach.

In an effort to force his way into the meeting where he was being accused and "tried" without benefit of a

21

court, Smith was challenged by Reid, on guard at the entrance to the causeway. Bullets flew; both men fell to the deck mortally wounded. Smith died almost immediately. Reid hung on for 12 days before passing away in the Bishop Rowe Hospital.

Reid is credited with the shooting of Smith, but there were many who claim he was shot from ambush and that the bullets taken from his body did not match up in caliber with Reid's borrowed weapon. Reid, however, was the hero of the day and was honored with the largest funeral in Skagway's history. A large marble marker was placed over his grave. Smith's grave, dug some 6 feet outside of the cemetery boundary so as not to "desecrate the hallowed

Monument erected at the grave of Frank Reid following his fatal duel with Soapy Smith is located in the pioneer cemetery, only a few feet from the grave of the man who shot him. The stone is engraved with the words, "He gave his life for the Honor of Skagway."

HOWARD CLIFFORD

Part of the crowd which attended Frank Reid's funeral. Services were held in the church on the right. Smith was a large contributor when citizens started a fund drive to build the facility. It was Skagway's first church.

ground," was marked first with a plain wooden marker and later with a stone headpiece.

Robert E. Sheldon Jr. was present at the shootout between Smith and Frank Reid. He was about 100 to 125 yards away at the time, and reported that he could see a heated argument was going on between the two, and that Soapy pointed his Winchester at Reid, who grabbed the barrel with his left hand and reached for his revolver with the right.

Soapy was the first to fire his weapon, Sheldon reported. (Most reports state that Reid pulled the trigger first, but that his pistol did not respond, giving Smith time to re-aim his rifle and wound Reid.) Despite being hit, Reid was able to fire three times, Sheldon reported, with each bullet leaving its mark on Soapy's body. Both collapsed on the dock.

Sheldon stated that it was a quiet evening and that there were not a great number of people about. As far as the report that possibly Smith was shot from ambush, Sheldon said he did not hear any other shots, and that if one had been fired, he was certain he would have heard it. Sheldon stated, "Later a White Pass employee, Willie Flynn, related the story to tourists that Smith was shot from ambush, but he was unable to substantiate the report."

Following the shooting of Soapy Smith, 26 persons were arrested by acting deputy marshal Josiah M. (Si) Tanner, who was sworn in after Deputy Taylor was removed from office for his close connection with the Smith operations. This number is a far cry from the several hundred who were supposed to be followers of Soapy. Of that number, 11 were bound over to the grand jury in Sitka and accompanied there by John Shook, a deputy marshal from Dyea. Nine were deported from town on the British steamer *Tartar*. The others were freed.

John Stewart returned to Nanaimo where he worked for a mining company until 1912. Following a series of study courses and examinations Stewart was appointed superintendent and instructor at the Government Mine Rescue Station and became recognized as an authority in such work in the Pacific Northwest. He remained in government service until his retirement at 65, and died in 1930 at the age of 84. Stewart's wife and two daughters predeceased him.

Soapy Smith's parlor was located at 317 Holly Street (Sixth Avenue) before it was moved a second time to its present location on the Skagway waterfront. Next to Smith's place is the original Skagway fire station, torn down several years ago.

HOWARD CLIFFORD

Marshal Tanner went into the hardware business in Skagway and remained there for many years. He was a member of the first Territorial legislature in 1913, and was appointed United States marshal for the First Judicial District on July 1, 1917. He served until September 1921, and died in Skagway 6 years later.

THE MILITARY
RESTORES ORDER

Following the killing of Soapy Smith, the so-called vigilantes got out of hand in their enthusiasm in rounding up suspected members of Smith's band. Two days later it was necessary for Commissioner Sehlbrede to call out the military stationed in Dyea to restore order in Skagway.

Capt. Richard T. Yeatman and a platoon of infantrymen arrived just in time to avert a hanging and to stop looting in the city. Order was restored and the troops returned to Dyea.

The military had received previous assignments in Alaska from the time of the purchase from Russia. Soldiers were on hand at Sitka in 1867 when the formal transfer took place, and troops were ordered to Alaska again during the gold rush. Royal North West Mounted Police were firmly entrenched at the summit of the passes, where a tentative boundary between the United States and Canada had been established.

Four companies of the 14th Cavalry from Vancouver Barracks in Washington State were sent to the communities at the head of Lynn Canal, with Companies B and H being assigned to Dyea under command of Col. Thomas McAnderson and Companies A and G, commanded by Lt. Col. George B. Russell, assigned to Skagway. Each command consisted of 4 officers and 108 men. The troops sailed from Portland on the *SS Undine* and arrived at Skagway February 25, 1898. There was an immediate need for their services, because the ship they were aboard was the center of a dock battle between longshoremen and a band of Juneau Indians on Captain Moore's Skagway wharf. The Indians had been imported by the Pacific Coast Steamship Company to break a longshore strike which had resulted from the reduction of wages, from 75 cents an hour to 50 cents an hour. The Indians were being paid only 25 cents an hour to unload ships and had put the longshoremen out of work.

The troops brought a quick halt to the melee and drove the longshoremen back, protecting the Indians while they continued the unloading. Later an

agreement was reached, for the longshoremen to handle the chores on the dock and the Indians to handle the cargo aboard the ships.

As is often the case with the military, the soldiers assigned to Skagway arrived in midwinter totally unprepared as far as outfitting was concerned. Instead of the coonskin caps, muskrat gloves and buffalo coats the regulars at other northern posts wore, these troops were outfitted in campaign hats, regulation blue overcoats, white cotton gloves and lightweight undergarments. They nearly froze to death, especially the company assigned to the post a mile and a half up the Skagway trail to keep order on the Brackett Wagon Road.

There was little for the military to do, and with the Spanish-American War at its peak a few months after

Skagway's gold rush cemetery has scores of graves of those who died on the trail, of illness during Skagway's harsh winter, or perhaps in a gun duel.

HOWARD CLIFFORD

27

the troops arrived, it was deemed best that the experienced military personnel in Skagway be withdrawn and sent to the front.

Although Soapy Smith had been turned down in his efforts to have the Skagway Guards accepted by the War Department for duty in the Spanish-American War, he was proud of the letter of commendation from the War Department he had received for his efforts and displayed it at his place of business. It never could be said that he was not patriotic.

When the troops from Skagway boarded the steamer *Queen* to go to Manila, there were only a few citizens on hand to see them off. Soapy learned of this and went into action. He entered the Theatre Royale, stopped the show and made a speech while standing in the aisle, stating that he wanted everyone down on the wharf to give the soldiers a proper sendoff. He gathered up the musicians from other theaters and dance halls, and the gamblers, dance-hall girls and customers alike all paraded down to the wharf. When the soldiers heard the band coming they crowded the rails of the ship. Needless to say, Soapy had requisitioned refreshments from the various saloons en route. For the 2 hours before the steamer pulled out, there was a hot old time on dock and aboard ship, so much so, in fact, that several prominent businessmen failed to find the gangplank to disembark when the ship sailed and got a free trip to Juneau, the next port of call.

Minor troubles kept the remaining troops at Dyea busy in other areas at times, and on one occasion they were called upon to handle the U.S. mail when citizens became upset over delays of more than 24 hours in transporting it between Dyea and Skagway.

Captain Yeatman and his troops were relieved after 15 months in Alaska on May 20, 1899, by Company L of the 24th Infantry, commanded by Capt. Henry W. Hovey. The unit was one of four black Regular Army units in existence at the time. It had an exceptional war record against the Indians and in the earlier days of the Spanish-American War.

Dyea had seen its best days by this time and the military quarters were in a sad state of repair. Captain Hovey was searching for other billets when a forest fire destroyed the facilities. Temporary headquarters were set up in a rented warehouse in Skagway and the troops were moved to property belonging to Captain Moore, who let them stay without charge. Later the troops moved into the Astoria Hotel, where the company was charged $175 a month.

One of the few occasions that there was need for the Skagway troops was an all-out encounter with striking White Pass & Yukon Route construction workers who, led by radicals, attempted to destroy the roundhouse and shops in town. The troops routed the strikers, the ring leaders were arrested and the gatherings of strikers in town were broken up. Within a short time workers were lining up to return to their jobs.

Although there was less for the black troops to do than there had been for the previous infantrymen, they remained in Skagway until 1902, when the 106th Company of the Coast Artillery from Fort Lawton, Seattle, relieved them. The 106th was later withdrawn and the only troops in the area were at Haines Mission (Fort William H. Seward which later became Chilkoot Barracks).

By 1925 Chilkoot Barracks was the only active post in Alaska, with 14 officers and 241 men. That remained the situation until the build-up for World War II, and the all-important job performed by the 770th Railroad Operating Battalion which took over operation of the White Pass & Yukon during the war. It did a most outstanding job against tremendous odds, as did the port embarkation companies and the hospital unit assigned to Skagway.

The railroaders were the last military personnel assigned to Skagway in any numbers. They, along with the construction workers from the Metcalf, Hamilton & Kansas City Bridge Companies (MHKCB), Bechtol-Price-Callahan and Elliott Co., all of which were active in wartime construction in the area, did much to liven things up on Saturday nights in the long-quiet town of Skagway.

CHURCHMEN ENTER THE PICTURE

The first man of the cloth to arrive in Skagway was a Presbyterian minister, the Reverend Robert McCahon Dickey, who landed on October 9, 1897, just as the town was entering into its most lawless period.

The next Sunday, October 11, saw the first religious services held in Burkhard Hall and those present decided to build a church. By the third Sunday only $200 had been contributed, far short of the amount needed to assure the start of a building. A concentrated fund drive was decided upon and in almost no time at all, thanks to a healthy boost from the much-maligned Soapy Smith, more than enough money was raised to assure the start of construction. In 2 months the building was completed and on December 12, 1897, the dedication of the Union Church took place. Initially four services were scheduled for the day, but when the Reverend Dickey learned that a Catholic priest had just arrived in town, a Roman Catholic service was also arranged.

The church was filled to overflowing as Father O'Neil and the Reverend Dickey walked down the aisle to the platform at 9 a.m. At 11 a.m. the church was again filled as the Right Reverend Peter T. Rowe, Episcopal Bishop for Alaska from Sitka, wearing the robes of his office, and the Reverend Dickey entered. Later in the day the actual dedication was held with representatives from seven denominations present, each pledging loyalty on behalf of his people.

The church was the center of Skagway's first Christmas, and the services were concluded with the presentation of a purse to the Reverend Dickey by the Ladies' Aid to help him with expenses he would have en route to the Yukon. When the Reverend Dickey went to the Klondike on April 1, 1898, after only 6 months in the community, he left behind him in Skagway a church which also served as a school, a community hospital, humane society and a club for both men and women.

The hospital was founded on February 19, 1898, by a group of townspeople under the Reverend Dickey's

Rev. Robert McCahon Dickey (left), first man of the cloth to arrive in Skagway, and Skagway's first church and school. Reverend Dickey, a Presbyterian minister, was in Skagway for only 6 months, but during that period, he was instrumental in constructing the church, which also served as a school, as well as the community's first hospital. In April 1898, he headed over the White Pass to the Klondike. He is pictured here with Reverend Grant (right) and other missionaries who traveled over the pass ahead of him.

HEGG PHOTO FROM THE UNIVERSITY OF WASHINGTON LIBRARY

direction, to meet the emergency of the great epidemic of spinal meningitis that swept the region. The largest log cabin in town—some 16 by 24 feet—was purchased with funds raised by subscription, and a nurse was hired to take care of patients the best she could. Able assistance came from townsfolk, including many of the girls from the dance halls who did yeoman work in caring for the sick through the epidemic.

So great was the emergency that not even beds were provided. Patients were attended while lying side by side on the floor. Others died unknown and uncared for in their tents and cabins.

One of several doctors in Skagway, one of the few remembered today, was Dr. Will H. Chase, who served one and all during the meningitis epidemic. He also was one of the first to aid the injured in the big slide at Sheep Camp. Later he went to Dawson and the Klondike, but returned to Alaska and served more than 20 terms as mayor of the city of Cordova while practicing medicine in that community. In his later years he became quite an author, with several books to his credit.

Following the departure of the Reverend Dickey for the Klondike, Bishop Rowe was asked to assume charge and ownership of the hospital. With the stipulation that he make an immediate outlay of $1,000 in improving the facility, title to the cabin and lot was turned over to him. Bishop Rowe spent more than $3,000 improving the hospital and added a two-story frame building next to the original structure.

The hospital was put under direction of Miss Duley, Miss Carter and their associates. The Reverend M. Wooden, who was appointed to the staff in 1898, was transferred to the Yukon in 1899, with the Reverend James G. Cameron appointed to succeed him. The Bishop Rowe Hospital was closed in 1905 because there was no further need for it. The newer White Pass & Yukon Route facility was well able to serve the community.

Bishop Rowe had visited the Skagway area before the gold rush. He was appointed the first Bishop of Alaska for the Episcopal Church following his consecration in New York in 1895. In the spring of 1896, with one companion he packed over the Chilkoot Pass on his first visit to the Interior. His district ranged from Ketchikan on the south to Point Barrow on the north, and from British Columbia to the Aleutians. No hardship was too great, no winter too cold and no trail too long to turn the bishop from his work of officiating as teacher, physician, jurist and priest through his territory. Bishop Rowe was known and welcomed on the trail. His fame spread, and it got around that he didn't haul out the Bible to minister to hungry sourdoughs. He offered them, instead, a bowl of hot mulligan.

Realizing that many of the people he needed to reach were more likely found in the saloons

Opposite—*Rt. Rev. Peter T. Rowe, Episcopal Bishop of Alaska. Bishop Rowe played an important role in the development of the Bishop Rowe Hospital in Skagway, and was welcomed by sourdoughs wherever they met, whether it be on the trail, in a saloon or in church.*

CURTIS & MINNER PHOTO
FROM WASHINGTON STATE HISTORICAL SOCIETY

of Skagway, Bishop Rowe frequently startled the Sunday morning bar regulars. There was something about the bishop's big shoulders and his glinting eyes that quieted the crowd when he preached, leaning against the bar. When the bishop bowed his head to pray, the sourdoughs, after a glance around, followed suit.

Bishop Rowe had his share of problems with his dogs, as did many others. Once when he was breaking in a new team the dogs fell through the thin ice. After much hard work, he got them out. When asked what he had been saying as he struggled to free them, his reply was, "God knows, the dogs know and I know. No one else is ever going to know."

The Catholic residents of Skagway were first visited from Douglas Island by the Reverend Paul Gougis, S. J., with Mass celebrated in private homes. Missionary work officially started in Skagway on September 8, 1898, when the Reverend Philbert H. Turnell, S. J., arrived. Three months later, Father John B. Rene, S. J., purchased a large empty store and converted it into a church. St. Mark's Church, located in the central part of Skagway, was dedicated on Christmas Eve, 1898, and was filled to capacity for midnight Mass.

Early in the spring of 1898 the Reverend A. J. Campbell arrived and founded the first Episcopal church. He was succeeded by the Reverend L. J. H. Wooden.

In May 1898, the Reverend Latourette, a Baptist missionary, came to Skagway and remained until August, when he was succeeded by the Reverend J. C. Jordan.

The Reverend W. J. Leach, Methodist-Episcopal, came in July 1898 and remained until September when he was succeeded by the Reverend Sprague Davis.

The Salvation Army entered the picture in April 1898 when a party of officers, headed by Evangeline Booth, daughter of the founder of the Army, arrived on the *SS Tees* out of Vancouver. The band marched from the ship to the center of town to the tune of *Onward Christian Soldiers*. The first meeting was held at Holly (Sixth) and Broadway, between Soapy Smith's saloon and the Pack Train Inn, and Soapy was one of those in attendance, observing the service from the edge of the crowd. Later he met Miss Booth and aided her efforts in the community.

The Army rented a vacant store on Broadway and held regular services for many years until the town went dry during prohibition.

The Young Men's Christian Association was also active in Skagway during the early days of the rush. One project of the 12-member board of directors was a reading room open to all. There was also a women's auxiliary. Total membership was more than 1,000 at the turn of the century.

THE POSTAL SERVICE

When men get far from home and their loved ones, one of the most urgent needs is letters and news from home. It was the lack of such word that caused many to leave Skagway and the Klondike, not the hardships of the trail. Concern for their families sent them back.

Mail was handled in a rather haphazard manner in the early days. The nearest post office was in Juneau, and pursers from the ships carried letters on to men known to be in Skagway. There Dr. Harry Runnalls made himself postmaster by the simple expedient of meeting each steamer and getting the mail from the purser. He distributed the mail from the small tent which also served as his office. Later the doctor moved into a small shack, and as the town grew, so did the mail lines whenever a steamer arrived in port. Dr. Runnalls charged up to 25 cents a letter for his postal service.

The first U.S. Post Office was opened November 10, 1897, with William B. Sampson as postmaster. There was high hope the service would be improved, but that was not the case. Newspapers were looked upon as unimportant as far as the post office was concerned and were lost or destroyed. Mail was brought only on the Pacific Coast Steamship Company's boats, which were considered most reliable. When a boat came in, three or four men were needed to distribute the mail, but since Skagway was only a fourth-class post office, the salary was not adequate for even one man. Understandably, service was poor.

On mail day the post office would allow a few of those in line to receive their mail, then would close its doors so remaining mail might be sorted. Then the

Opposite—*Skagway settlers line up at the office of Dr. Harry Runnalls waiting for their mail. Dr. Runnalls was Skagway's first unofficial postmaster.*

doors were opened to another small group. One observer pointed out that it was not uncommon to stand 3 or 4 hours in the cold, muddy street before one reached the postal window.

Indifferent clerks would look through the letters under one's initial, and after stating that there was no mail, would put the letters back in the wrong pigeonholes. If any complaint was uttered about the mistakes, the sharp reply would be, "If you don't like our way of doing this, you had better come in here and do it yourself." Many a gold seeker went his way thinking the folks back home had forgotten him.

After the first few days of rushing business following the arrival of the mail boat, the post office would be deserted for perhaps 2 or 3 weeks until another mail boat arrived. Following the establishment of the post office, Dr. Runnalls, who had been a physician for the Royal North West Mounted Police, continued as the town's leading physician. Together with other business leaders, he established the first power plant and water system, the Skagway Light and Water Co. Later he returned to his home in Puyallup, Washington.

Another utility project, Alaska Light and Power Co., had Charles R. Hurley, president; Chester Thorne, secretary and treasurer; and W. G. Gaston, general manager. Thorne returned to Tacoma, Washington, where he commissioned Alaskan Indians from Sitka to carve a totem pole which for some 65 years was the "world's tallest." It was topped a few years ago by carvers at Haines-Port Chilkoot under the direction of Carl Heinmiller. The new Alaska-carved pole was first displayed in Japan at Expo '70 and then brought back to Alaska and erected at the village of Kake, in the Southeastern part of the state.

Following Sampson as postmaster was Augustus E. Kindell, who took over on May 20, 1905. As the years

Opposite—*Early day photo of Skagway showing the line-up of Klondikers awaiting their mail. The mail at that time was handled by Dr. Harry Runnalls, a Canadian who charged a small fee for delivery to the addressees. Later the U.S. Postal Service took over, and service became worse, according to early day records.*

ASAHEL CURTIS PHOTO FROM UNIVERSITY OF WASHINGTON

passed, the service began to improve. Sampson was in the position for more than 10 years and was succeeded by Martin Conway on January 7, 1916, and by Conway's son John on January 12, 1930. Both Conways played important roles in the development of Skagway. Martin, a native of Ireland, stopped off in New York for a couple of years on the way to San Francisco where he worked in the City of Paris dry goods store, still in operation in that city.

In early 1897 he waited on a customer who was purchasing stock for his store in Juneau. Martin Conway showed much interest in this new land, and when the order was completed the customer, B. M. Behrends, invited him to come North to work in his new store. Behrends is still a major retail outlet in Juneau.

A year later Behrends decided to open a Skagway branch and selected young Conway to run it. A couple of years later Conway bought the property and ran it as a men's clothing store under the name of Martin Conway. On January 8, 1903, Martin married Rae Quinlan, who had been at Bennett and Carcross during the building of the White Pass & Yukon, and was keeping house in Skagway for her brother, Jerry Quinlan, the first conductor for the railroad. Three children were born to the couple, all in Skagway—Bess in November 1903, Jack in August 1905, and Martin Jr., in 1907. All attended school in Skagway, with Bess and Martin eventually going to Seattle to high school. Martin Jr. died of an illness while in Seattle. As the gold rush boom subsided, Martin Conway liquidated the store and in 1905 accepted an appointment as U.S. commissioner and probate judge in Skagway. In 1913 he was appointed postmaster by President Woodrow Wilson. He continued to serve in this position until his death in January 1930.

Meanwhile Jack had attended the University of Washington, receiving his degree in 1927. He spent summer vacations working on the White Pass and assisted his father in the post office. Upon the death of Martin Sr., Jack was appointed postmaster and served until 1933. In October 1930 he married Gertrude McGrath and later moved to Sitka where he became prominent in business.

The senior Mrs. Conway passed away several years ago at the age of 92.

William H. Murray took over as Skagway's acting postmaster on April 11, 1933, and after serving through several administrations was followed by Marshall V. Rafferty. Others who served included Hazel May Benedict, Alice F. Selmar, Lawrence T. McGuane and Jack C. Lee.

AND THE NEWSPAPERS

With newspapers handled the way they were by the post office, it was only natural that local publications would spring to life in order to relay the news to the thousands of prospectors and others who were in Skagway. The first of several newspapers was the *Skaguay News,* established as a weekly on October 15, 1897, with M. L. Sherpy as editor and publisher. This was a four-page publication and one of the most popular in the area, due largely to the efforts of associate editor Elmer J. (Stroller) White, one of the best-known of the early day editors in the North.

White was considered a combination Will Rogers and Art Buchwald of his time. He wrote columns before there was such a thing as a recognized columnist. Always a wanderer, White came from Ohio, where he was born in 1859. He graduated from Muskingum College at New Concord, Ohio, and began newspapering with the *Gainesville News* in Florida. He worked for papers in the South, and made his way to the Puget Sound area where he worked from 1891 to 1898 and then headed for the Klondike.

His work with the *Skaguay News* at the time Soapy Smith was at his height enabled him to savor the strange society of a kind of people who amused and fascinated him. He could cover the news with the best of them, but mostly wrote for the fun of it. The subjects of his pieces were the motley ne'er-do-wells, hard drinkers, gamblers, bartenders, dance-hall girls and just plain bums who contributed little of value but much in the way of color to life in Skagway, Dawson and the North. As he put it, he liked to write about the Sam brothers—Flot and Jet.

SKAGUAY, ALASKA, JULY 8, 1898.

Soapy Smith's Last Bluff
And Its Fatal Ending.

rmed With a Winchester He Endeavors to Intimidate a Large Meeting of Indignant Citizens on the Juneau Wharf

OT THROUGH THE HEART BY FRANK REID.

e Jail Nearly Full of Members of "Soapy's" Gang, and Citizens Armed with Winchesters Still Rounding Them Up. Brave Frank Reid will Probably Recover. The Inquest.

Soapy" Smith is dead! Shot ugh the heart, his cold body n a slab at People's undertak- rlors, and the confidence men unco steerers which have had headquarters here for some have suddenly taken their de- re, the tragic death of their r having completely unnerved

was at 9:30 last night that the kered career of "Soapy" Smith brought to a sudden end by a libre bullet from a revolver in erring right hand of City Sur- Frank H. Reid, while the lies at the hospital dangerous- unded by a bullet from Smith's

cause which led up to the to which ended Smith's life,

ward demonstrations were made, although there was an ominous look worn by several hundred of men, including the foreman of the News office, who sug- gested the election of a chairman, Thomas Whitten of the Golden North hotel, being chosen. The chairman appointed a committee of four. Frank H. Reid, Jesse

chesters, are congregated on the streets, but the best of order prevails.

Four deputy Marshals, Caswell, Joy, Barney and another, were sent over the trail to Lake Bennett this morning in search of the notorious three who stole the bag of gold. Joy is an ex-detective, from New York and smart as a whip. Cas- well is equally as brave, and when they return it is safe to say that they will render a good account of themselves.

THE DEAD MAN'S FAMILY.

Although there was not a single person in Skaguay who appeared to do honor to the man who yesterday was a popular hero and is to day but a dead highway- man, yet there are those who will deep- ly mourn his untimely end. Smith re- ceived on the last mail photographs of his wife and 6 children, who are living at St. Louis, also loving letters from them. Smith was born at Camilla, Ga., 48 years ago, and has a brother who is one of the

KLONDIKE GOLD
COMES OUT THIS WAY

Skaguay's Bank and Hotel Safes Stuffed with Golden Dust and Yellow Nuggets

THIS ROUTE BEATS THEM ALL.

It is Only Ten Days via Bennett to Seattle, versus Twenty-Six Days, bar accident, by Way of St. Michaels.

HIP, HIP, HURRAH! Gee whiz!! A goodly part of this season's output of gold from the Klondike will undoubted- ly come out this way! About a quarter of a million of it came out this way yes- terday, and this was merely by way of experiment. The men who carried the precious metal started from Dawson by steamboat, but whether they would be able to navigate in these steamers as far as the White Horse rapids, and then to make connection with other steamers to Lake Bennett, was a question that even the steamboat operators were unable to guarantee.

But the experiment proved a success, and last night there was more excite- ment over the arrival of some forty Klondikers with good news from the interior, and with bags of nuggets and dust to prove it, than could be expected even on a railroad pay day.

On June 24 and 28 two upper Yukon river boats started from Dawson, or rather some mile or so above Dawson, as the river bank of that famous Mecca was so thickly studded with all sorts of craft that a steamboat was unable to put

on the 28th, the Goddard left, and overtook its competitor at that point. The Kilborne started from Bennett on Tuesday and brought up the passengers of both boats the following day.

Some of these came in last night via Dyea, but the majority over the Skaguay wagon road. Of the former 3 old timers, headed by Jim Mc- Intire, called at the old stopping place before Skaguay was; Healy & Wilson's store, and there deposited 150 pounds of gold dust and nuggets. Five of their companions also depos- ited their dust in Sam Heron's safe.

Another party coming out consisted of C. P. Devine, Tacoma; W. H. Snyder, Fort Wayne; H. O. Kenyon, J. Brennan, Chas. H. Tate, John Anderson, M. Vieira and Jos. Mendes. Each of these men showed a bucksikin sack of pet nug- gets, but as to the amounts of their piles they were all reticent. A second party of 8 came to Skaguay direct from Sheep Camp, and it re- quired two large boats to bring the men and their precious stuff over.

The First Bank of Skaguay kept open late last night to receive in their time care the dust brought in by the Yukoners, and all the safes of the hotels in the city were utilized. The brothers Butler, of Lexington, Ky., pre- ferred to keep their dust in sight all the time, and when they went over to the Pack Train restaurant from the Hotel Astoria, where they were staying, they carried their winnings with them. Richard Butler, the Captain of the team has been in for two years, and sent for his

After a short stint with the *Skaguay News,* White moved on to Dawson and more fertile fields in November 1898. Many of his columns from the Juneau and Douglas papers, reminiscent of Skagway and Klondike days, have been published in book form under the title *Tales of a Klondike Newsman.*

White stayed in the North following the rush, and in 1918 was elected a member and later speaker of the House of Representatives of the Alaska Territorial Legislature. He became the first director of the Alaska Bureau of Publicity, but continued his interest in newspapering and at the time of his death in 1930, was publishing *Stroller's Weekly.* His wife published the paper for a time after his death. Mount Stroller White near Juneau is an enduring monument to one of the great writers spawned by the Klondike gold rush.

Opposite—*Reproduction of the front page of* The Skaguay News, *covering the story of Soapy Smith's death in a gun duel with Frank Reid.*

HOWARD CLIFFORD COLLECTION

After White's departure from Skagway, Joseph T. Hayne took over as editor and publisher of the *News* from 1901 to 1902. The publication was discontinued in 1903.

Another paper of the time was the *Daily Alaskan,* which was established on February 1, 1898. It was published each evening except Sunday, but later became a morning publication. Oscar W. Dunbar was the initial publisher, but sold out in a couple of months to George W. DeSuca. The paper was described as each issue being "chuck-a-block with fresh, crisp, newsy reading matter, and its advertising patronage speaks in no uncertain tone the high regard in which it is held by the business community."

Dr. Allan Hornsby became editor at the time of the DeSuca takeover, but was requested to leave town in July 1898 as a result of his close association with Jefferson Randolph Smith.

Other editors under the DeSuca ownership were many, and included John W. Troy from Port Townsend, Washington, who edited the *Daily Alaskan* from sometime in 1898 until 1907. Then Dr. L. S. Keller bought it from I. M. Jensen, who with

THE POPULAR HOTEL DEWEY.

e only hotel of Skaguay that is ded with steam heat is the Hotel y, situated on the corner of 7th ue and State street. The Dewey three story building, recently ructed and well furnished ghout, all its rooms being com- ous and richly furnished. hough conducted on the European plan arrangements are made for gues by which meals can be served in the rooms from near by restaurants. connection with the Dewey are th only Turkish baths operated in th city. Carriages running especially fo the Dewey meet all boats and train and are at all times at the disposal the guests of the house.

One Price Clothiers, FOURTH AN STATE

George S. Town had purchased the paper from DeSuca in December 1901. Dr. Keller was editor and publisher until his death in 1923.

Troy had served as deputy county auditor of Clallam County in Washington prior to coming to Skagway. He had founded the *Weekly Democratic Leader* in Port Townsend in 1891 and published it until 1897.

Troy also served as city clerk in Skagway, but returned to Seattle in 1907 to become a publicity agent. Four years later he founded the *Alaska-Yukon Magazine* and published it for a year, only to return to Alaska in 1913 as editor of the *Daily Alaska Empire* in Juneau. A year later he purchased the paper. In 1919 he was appointed collector of customs for the District of Juneau, a position he held until 1922.

In 1933 he was appointed governor of the Territory by President Franklin D. Roosevelt, and served until 1939 when he resigned due to ill health. He retired to private business and died May 2, 1942, in Juneau.

After Oscar Dunbar sold the *Daily Alaskan* he founded the *Skagway-Atlin Budget* in 1898. The *Budget* was published as a morning paper by the Skagway Printing and Publishing Co. until it was absorbed into the *Alaska Daily Guide* (also known as the *Alaska Travelers' Guide*) which was founded in 1900 and published daily except Monday by the Alaska-Yukon Publishing Co. Dunbar became its editor. O. M. Kinney later published the *Alaska-Yukon Mining Journal*, a monthly published from February 1901 until April 1902. The *Guide* was published until April 30, 1905.

In 1898 a lone issue of the *War Bulletin* was printed, carrying the news of the Spanish-American War "for all from Skagway to Dawson City." J. G. Proctor was editor. One thousand copies were printed, and a large number were taken to Dawson where they were sold for $1.50 a copy.

Other publications sprang up, and as the gold rush waned, died in short order. Skagway settled back to being a small, quiet community. Skagway's newspaper today is *The North Wind*, founded in 1963 and published by Cy Coyne on a monthly basis.

ENTERTAINMENT: GOOD, BAD & INDIFFERENT

Skagway by the summer of 1898 had become a city of some 15,000 persons living in tents, shacks and improvised rooming houses. Lawlessness and disorder continued but in a somewhat different form following the demise of Soapy and his followers.

There were 61 saloons, as many gambling dives, plus a number of small adjoining dance nooks where maids and men amused themselves in far-from-innocent frolic. Dance-hall queens such as Sitting Maude, the Montana Filly, Ethel the Moose, Sweet Marie, the Oregon Mare, Molly Fewclothes, The Virgin, Diamond Lil Davenport, Babe Wallace and many others were making Skagway their headquarters.

In Skagway the art of "box rushing" was developed into a highly efficient operation of separating the customer from his ready cash. The female singers and dancers, once the show was completed, rushed into boxes demanding drinks, ordering champagne at $20

a pint and up from the waiters, who were thugs unwise to disappoint. Naturally the customer paid, and paid and paid.

One such place, the Bonanza, was visited by a packtrain contractor, Joe Brooks, who was engaged in hauling supplies for the Royal North West Mounted Police at Lake Bennett. At the end of the evening the proprietor gave him a $4,700 bill. He paid $750 for a box of cigars and nearly $3,000 for drinks for himself and an "uninvited" female companion, but he balked at the additional $1,000 tacked on the bill.

The proprietor of the resort appealed to Colonel Steele at the police barracks at Bennett, and was promptly ordered out and warned if he ever crossed the line into Canada again he would be arrested.

There was no economic necessity for a girl of talent to augment her income in such a manner, because there was a constant demand for good entertainers in the variety theaters at $150 a week. Singers such as Anna Kane (The Nightingale of the North), Nellie LaMarr, Minnie LaTour, Blanche LaMonte and Jessie LaVore (it was the French period in vaudeville) were on stage in Skagway.

Entertainers bound for the Klondike.

There were also the usual specialty acts—knife throwers, acrobats, trained dog acts, dancing bears, magicians and tumblers. Names such as Lady Godiva, Calamity Jane, Little Egypt (famous in the Chicago World's Fair of 1893) and others were prominent on the theater billboards.

Another favorite at the music halls, who arrived in Skagway at an early age and was content to entertain for what loose change was tossed his way, was Eddie Peabody, better known in later years as "King of the Banjo." Eddie augmented his meager earnings by selling papers on street corners in the business section of town.

Irish tenors were also much in the limelight and most of the popular songs of the time had a ragtime air. There were *There'll Be A Hot Time in The Old Town Tonight; Down Went McGinty; Put Your Arms Around me, Honey; Ta-ra-ra Boom-de-ay,* as well as the more sentimental and slower-paced songs of Stephen Foster, *Genevieve, Bird in a Gilded Cage* and *After the Ball.*

Most of the top names who came to Skagway played at the Theatre Royale, owned by Dave Blake and operated by Boston Page. The 1,200-seat theater advertised that it was equipped with the latest in theater equipment and that it was a first-class, refined vaudeville house. Another entertainment center was the Lobby Music Hall on Sixth Avenue, owned by R. R. Mitchell. It was advertised as a "high-class resort, with good music and refreshments."

Female performers were divided roughly into three classifications—the ill-rewarded aristocracy of dramatic actresses, the flashier and much better-paid girls who sang and danced but would not mingle with the patrons as part of their duties and the variety girls who worked in the lower-class music halls and drank "on a percentage" with customers after their turn on stage.

There was also the "line" where the out-and-out professionals worked. This area attracted such as Mattie Silks, most notorious madame of Denver's Holladay Street, as well as others from the infamous Barbary Coast of San Francisco.

KIRMSE'S JEWELRY

With its breweries, bars and brothels doing a rip-roaring business, Skagway in the early days was described by Superintendent Samuel B. Steele of the Royal North West Mounted Police as probably "the roughest place in the world, little better than a hell on earth."

Skagway had its more legitimate side also. There were many who seriously entered into the acceptable roads of commerce.

One such was Herman D. Kirmse, who in 1897 opened a jewelry and watch-repair shop in a tent he shared with a cobbler. Kirmse, born in Dubuque, Iowa, a descendant of a European family which for several hundred years had produced many outstanding jewelers, watchmakers and doctors, came to Skagway after having followed every gold rush and silver rush from Colorado to South Dakota. His Skagway business prospered, and shortly thereafter he opened

Herman Kirmse, one of Skagway's pioneer businessmen, is pictured at the turn of the century. Kirmse established one of the town's first jewelry and watchmaking stores, which is operated by the family today. It is located at Fifth and Broadway.

COURTESY OF MR. AND MRS. JACK KIRMSE

49

the Pioneer Jewelry Store across the street from the present Kirmse Jewelry and Curio Store on Broadway.

Always alert to opportunity, Kirmse in 1898 led a group of Indian packers over Chilkoot Pass with the first window glass to be brought into the Klondike. After reaching Bennett a barge was constructed and the glass taken downriver, through the treacherous White Horse Rapids to Dawson City. Here Kirmse sold the 7- by 9-inch panes for as much as $2 each. On another occasion Kirmse, recognizing the need for fresh fruit and vegetables in the Klondike, took a shipment of cantaloupes over the pass and down the river to Dawson, selling the bruised and damaged ones for $20 each and the firm, good ones for up to $50 each. The money gained from these ventures was invested in gold claims, mining property and the grub-staking of prospectors, without satisfactory financial return.

Later in 1898 Kirmse was commissioned by one of the town's better-known gamblers, Pat Renwick, to make a nugget watch chain from 10 of the largest nuggets that had come out of the Klondike and which Renwick had won at his faro table. This chain, which weighed approximately 3 pounds, was used by Renwick through the years as collateral for funds to support his gambling operations. They were "pawned" and "redeemed" with Kirmse as often as three times a day.

Oftentimes Herman Kirmse was elsewhere than in his store and although for a short time he had a partner, Frank Lowe, who later opened a furniture store with Martin Sickenger, it was necessary for Renwick to search Kirmse out in order to "borrow" or "repay." Finally Kirmse set up an arrangement whereby funds were placed in a cigar box in the store's safe, which was left open to enable the gambler to pick up the money needed, leaving the nugget chain as

Opposite—*Built as a jewelry store at the turn of the century by Herman Kirmse, the business is operated today by his son Jack. The other half of the store was the home of the Pioneer Cigar Factory. Next door was the Seattle Headquarters Saloon, with the Occidental Hotel occupying the two upper floors. The Kelley Drug Co. occupied the other large building, constructed in 1904.*

HOWARD CLIFFORD

security. As his luck changed, Renwick would replace the funds and redeem the nuggets.

This policy continued for 11 years, and when Renwick passed away in 1909 the nugget chain was in the cigar box. Kirmse paid Renwick's widow the difference between the "loan" and the value of the chain and it has remained in possession of the Kirmse family ever since.

In 1900 Herman Kirmse, a widower with one daughter, married Hazel Cleveland, beautiful daughter of a prominent Juneau pioneer family who had moved to Skagway. Two sons, Jack and Dan, were born to the couple. Kirmse's jewelry creations in gold, gold nuggets, Alaskan ivory and silver became world renowned and were awarded four gold and three bronze medals at the Alaska-Yukon-Pacific Exposition in Seattle in 1909.

Shortly thereafter Kirmse opened a branch store in Ketchikan, Alaska's first city, and it was while visiting there in 1912 that he met a tragic accidental death as he slipped and fell from the city dock while greeting friends on a visiting steamer. Mrs. Kirmse later remarried and sold the Ketchikan outlet, but

HOWARD CLIFFORD

Above—*The oldest frame building in Skagway is this home, formerly owned and occupied by Capt. Billy Moore, founder of the community. The property was purchased by Herman Kirmse, and has been the home of the Kirmse family since the early days in Skagway. The home has been remodeled and is owned by Mr. and Mrs. Jack Kirmse. Opposite—Ben Moore (right), son of the founder of Skagway, and his daughter with their pet moose, which was an early day attraction in Skagway. The photo was taken in front of the Moore home.*

DEDMAN'S PHOTO SHOP

continued to operate the store in Skagway with the assistance of her oldest son Jack until her death in 1962. Jack Kirmse and his wife Georgette have continued the store since, celebrating in 1972 the 75th anniversary of the founding in 1897. The present store on Broadway was constructed in 1899.

The Kirmse home is located on property, part of the original Captain Moore tract, which they purchased in 1910. Their Skagway home is the first frame house constructed in the city, in 1896 by Captain Moore. Next to it is the first Moore cabin which was moved to its present location from the original site, several hundred feet away.

AND WOMEN ARRIVE

Alaska, especially during the mad, hectic days of the gold rush, was considered strictly a man's country. Yet there was one woman who met the challenge of the frontier North when the gold fever hit and succeeded against overwhelming odds. That woman was Mrs. Harriet Pullen, founder and proprietor of the famous Pullen House Hotel, long one of Skagway's major attractions.

Left with a bankrupt farm in Washington State and four youngsters to rear when her husband died in 1895, Mrs. Pullen joined the gold rush and arrived in Skagway on September 8, 1897, on the steamer *Rosalie*, with only $7 and a few personal belongings.

She went to work in a tent "restaurant" so small that she couldn't stand upright to work. This was the beginning of her long career of catering to the public. Her initial customers were loggers getting out piling for a dock. Her apple pies, baked from dried apples in pie tins she pounded out of tin cans, started her on her way to success. Soon she moved to a log cabin and was

Opposite—*Pells and Feero packtrain prepares to leave Skagway for the summit of White Pass in 1898. Professional packers became some of the most prosperous of Skagway residents during the early days of the rush, but were put out of business with the construction of the White Pass & Yukon Route.*

WASHINGTON STATE HISTORICAL SOCIETY

Opposite—A prospector makes his way over the White Pass Trail accompanied by his dog and leading a pair of packhorses. The going was extremely rough over the trail, which was to become the Brackett Wagon Road and later the White Pass & Yukon Route. Above—The White Pass Trail was used summer and winter to haul supplies to the Klondike. The horse is hauling three loaded freight sleds over the summit, a total weight of some 1,400 pounds. At no time was there natural feed for the horses in the mountains, and during the winter there was no water.

able to send for her three sons, electing to leave her young daughter with friends in Washington. During the short-lived Atlin stampede she joined hundreds of others taking part in that rush, but soon returned to her restaurant in Skagway.

Packing Klondike freight over the White Pass Trail at outlandish prices was one of the best and fastest ways to prosperity in Skagway's hectic gold rush days in 1897-98. Mrs. Pullen still owned seven horses from her farm days at Cape Flattery in Washington and she sent for them with the thought of going into the packing business.

When the horses arrived she could not find anyone to bring them ashore from the ship in the harbor—the Skagway pier still was not completed—so she swam each one from the ship to the beach herself, unloading them from the ship by having them jump overboard, and then leading them to shore from her rowboat. She had grown up with horses and she understood and loved them. During the months she operated her packtrain and later drove a team to earn $25 a day, she proved her horsemanship many times over. She had only one animal injured, despite the fact that hundreds of horses died on the tortuous trail. Later she sold her outfit to one of the better-known operators on the trail.

As she prospered, and as Skagway became a more stable community following the establishment of law and order and the completion of the White Pass & Yukon, Mrs. Pullen rented a large house from Captain Moore and started a boarding house. It lacked furniture, and first boarders "roughed it" with furniture made from packing crates, apple boxes and the like, until she was able to lease furniture that had been sent North for a dance hall and was stored in a local warehouse.

Right—An early day photo of Mrs. Harriet "Mother" Pullen in Indian attire. This costume as well as others she wore on special occasions were sold at auction with the Pullen House Museum artifacts in Seattle in 1973. Opposite—The Pullen House Hotel and the Pullen House stage, driven by Mrs. Pullen. The Pullen House was one of Skagway's earliest and finest hotels, and was visited by many of the world's most famous people of the day. The Pullen House is located on Spring Street.

58

Later she purchased the building. The Pullen House became Skagway's finest hotel and was enlarged several times. The famous and the near-famous made it their headquarters in the North. It was the first, and for many years the only hotel in Alaska that offered fresh milk and cream. (Even in the late 1960's many first-class hotels in Alaska still had canned condensed milk on the table for coffee and cereal.) Fresh vegetables were also on the bill of fare. These goodies came from Mrs. Pullen's ranch in the Dyea area.

During the visit of President Warren G. Harding in 1923, shortly before his death in San Francisco, he visited the Pullen House. A monument on the grounds commemorates the visit.

One of Mrs. Pullen's great delights was standing in front of a group of wide-eyed tourists, relating tales of the early days and how Soapy Smith fleeced the gold

Mrs. Harriet Pullen came to Skagway as a penniless widow and built the famed Pulled House Hotel into one of the best in the North.

HOWARD CLIFFORD COLLECTION

60

rush cheechakos. Her spiel telling of the shooting of Soapy was a stunner. According to her story, she was right on the dock and saw the whole thing happen. Her very dramatic account, with full gestures, of Soapy and Frank Reid lying there in their blood had such a magnetic effect on the tourists that they listened with mouths open, scarcely breathing, eyes glued on Mrs. Pullen.

All year long Mrs. Pullen met every boat as it docked in Skagway. In the summer, when hoards of tourists arrived, she was in her element. She was a first-class showman and pulled out all the stops to gain maximum effect. She told the story so many times that what was fact and what was fiction doubtlessly became confused in her own mind. The tourists, however, lapped it up and loved every minute of it. Her story of the shooting, *Soapy Smith, Bandit of Skagway,* is available in bookstores.

Mrs. Pullen's sons grew to manhood and also became outstanding citizens. Two of them, Dan and Royal, graduated from the University of Washington with honors. Dan became the first cadet from Alaska to be named to West Point. During World War I he

Harriet "Mother" Pullen became a legend during and following the gold rush. She is pictured wearing some of the many medals, insignia and badges acquired by her sons during World War I. Such was her attire when she met the tourist boats as they docked at Skagway.

was decorated by Gen. John J. Pershing for valor while serving as a colonel with the engineers. Royal also received citations for unusual bravery during the conflict. The third son Chester was drowned at Ketchikan on his way to his second year at the University.

Mrs. Pullen became known as the "Mother of the North" during her 50 years in Skagway. She died in Skagway August 9, 1947, a few days before her 87th birthday and was buried in a private plot near the Pullen House, where she wanted to be.

During her lifetime she gathered one of the finest private collections of historic artifacts of Alaskana to be seen anywhere. The collection was in possession of her granddaughter, Mary Pullen Kopanski of Seattle, Washington, and for years was exhibited at the Seattle Center. The summer of 1973 saw the collection go under the auctioneer's hammer when remodeling of the building which housed it resulted in the loss of exhibition space. Many of the items which had at one time belonged to Soapy Smith, and had come into possession of Mrs. Pullen through an apparent close association between the two, were returned to the

Smith family when Randolph J. Smith, Soapy's grandson, was a successful bidder for Soapy's possessions. #

BUILDERS, RESTAURANTS & PHOTOGRAPHERS

Skagway during the early days of the rush was a city that offered opportunity to many trades in addition to the usual "butcher, baker and candlestick maker." Architects and builders were in constant demand in an effort by the community to keep up with the need for housing and business locations. Construction went on literally around the clock.

One of the first architects and builders to arrive was E. J. Liddicoat, who came to Skagway from Astoria, Oregon, in September 1897 and immediately became engaged in designing and building business houses

A Skagway street in 1897. One of the early day hotels, Samson's, is pictured along with a saloon, restaurant and cigar store.

ASAHEL CURTIS PHOTO
FROM WASHINGTON STATE HISTORICAL SOCIETY

and residences, some of which are still landmarks today. Five months later, on February 12, 1898, his wife and three daughters, Frances, Edith and Louise, joined him in Skagway. Two more children were born to the couple.

During the early days of the rush the Herman Richter family, consisting of Mr. and Mrs. Richter and their two sons, passed through Skagway en route to Dawson City. They met with little success in the Yukon and returned to Skagway in 1904. Herman Richter took over the U.S. Hotel on Second Avenue and operated the facility until 1911 when the elder Richters returned to Tacoma, Washington.

In 1910 the oldest of the Liddicoat girls, Frances, married one of the Richter boys, Emil H., in Skagway. Both worked in the jewelry store of P. E. Kern, and having learned the trade, opened their own store a year later. The business prospered and in 1922 they moved to the present Richter location on Broadway near Second. In 1929 they added to the store.

The Emil Richters had four children, two boys and two girls. The oldest son worked on the White Pass & Yukon Route for 41 years before quitting, not yet old

Above—Skagway's main street, Broadway, looking northeast. The building on the right is the Richter Jewelry store. Across from it are the Washington Fruit Store; Canadian Pacific Railway office, now occupied by the Trail Bench; the Arctic Brotherhood building; the Alaska Steamship Co. building, now occupied by the Shamrock Music Store; another building since torn down; and the Golden North Hotel. Farther up the street are a bakery and the old Museum of '98. Opposite—Skagway in the summer of 1897. At the right is Clancy's Saloon, one of the popular meeting places in the community.

enough to retire. The youngest son, Edward, like his parents became a jeweler. The two girls married and moved Outside. Emil Richter passed away in September 1947 and Frances took over operation of the store and continued to run it until 1968 when she retired, selling out to her son, Edward, who operates the store today. Mrs. E. H. Richter, the longest-time resident of Skagway—she has lived in the community since 1898—still drops into the store to help out when there are a large number of cruise-ship tourists in town. She delights in relating stories about gold rush days.

Just as building of housing and business establishments was necessary for the community, so

Opposite—*Corner of Broadway and Holly Street (Sixth Avenue) in Skagway at the turn of the century. Note the railroad tracks down the center of Broadway in the foreground. The Hotel Mondamin was one of the most prominent hotels during the early days in Skagway. The small white building on the right just beyond the "McRae and Tailor" sign was Soapy's parlor.*

was the task of feeding the multitude who descended on the shores of Skagway Bay. Among the early businessmen who did their utmost to fill this void were Anton Stanish and Louis Ceovich, who wrestled several tons of restaurant equipment ashore on the beach in 1897. They secured a large tent and opened what was to become Skagway's and the North's best-known restaurant, the Pack Train Inn.

A few months after opening their tent restaurant the pair moved into the first commercial building to be built in town, sharing it with the Pack Train Saloon. The facility, constructed by George Rice, was located across Holly Street from the Hotel Mondamin. Stanish and Ceovich remained here for more than a dozen years, but as times changed, so did the center of the business section. Stanish and Ceovich also moved, but the restaurant in the new location never regained its former prominence and after a couple of years Tony, who had bought out his partner, closed the doors and moved to Oregon to take up farming. He found it was not the life for him. He returned to Alaska and established another popular eating emporium in Ketchikan.

The Pack Train Inn Saloon building is now located on Broadway, open to the public during the summer tourist season.

One of the North's most famous photo-historians was Eric A. Hegg. He hauled more than a ton of photo equipment over the pass and down the Yukon to Dawson City where he established a studio. While on the trail, Hegg used a darkroom fastened to a sled pulled by a herd of long-haired goats. He heated his developer to keep it from freezing, and purified water by filtering it through charcoal. Despite these

HEGG PHOTO FROM UNIVERSITY OF WASHINGTON

Opposite—The gold rush town of Skagway during January 1898. The town had a few wooden buildings, but still a number of tents. Below—Lightering supplies ashore at Skagway in 1897, prior to the construction of the various wharfs. Supplies were unloaded onto barges from the coastal steamers and then moved as close to shore as possible. From this point wagons and the like were used to haul supplies over the tide flats to dry land.

ASAHEL CURTIS PHOTO
FROM WASHINGTON STATE HISTORICAL SOCIETY

difficulties, Hegg's photos of the gold rush were considered to be the most complete history of the Trail of '98. His Skagway studios now house the Dedman's Photo Shop.

At the time the gold fever hit, Hegg was the proprietor of two prosperous but small studios in the Bellingham, Washington, area. He had arrived in the Pacific Northwest in 1888, and had photographed much of that region's growing cities, scenic mountains, cascading streams, industry and people. Following the rush at Dawson City, Hegg rode a paddle-wheel steamer down the Yukon to the Bering Sea and was on the beaches of Nome when prospectors were panning for gold there. He remained in the North for some 20 years before returning to

Opposite—*Broadway in the early 1900's looking southwest. By this time the WP&YR tracks were running up the middle of the street, and the Golden North Hotel had been moved to Broadway from its original location. The square tower on the left is the Pack Train Inn building. The Board of Trade restaurant and saloon (on the right) had moved from Sixth.*

The old E. A. Hegg photo studios, now occupied by Dedman's Photo Shop, is seen on the right. The next building is one formerly occupied by Weed and Co., fruit and vegetables, and then the old Idaho Saloon. The photo was taken from near Fourth and Broadway looking toward the waterfront.

HOWARD CLIFFORD

Bellingham. He sold his properties there in 1946 and moved to California.

Asahel Curtis, one of the best-known photographers of the Pacific Northwest, also recorded the history of the period in Skagway, on the Trail and in the Klondike. He operated under much the same handicaps as did Hegg.

Shea & Patton was another photo outfit which did much work in Skagway, and had probably the most complete set of photos of Soapy Smith and his activities there. They were published in a 1907 Skagway booklet entitled *The Soapy Smith Tragedy*. The popular booklet has recently been republished and is available in bookstores.

Other photographers who passed through Skagway included Dobbs and Nowell, Duclos and Larss, and Winter and Pond, who were early on the scene, along with Blankenship. W. H. Case and his partner, Draper, settled in town. H. C. Barley photographed construction of the railroad.

A CLEAN START

A woman of the "line" gave George Dedman his start in Skagway in the laundry business. With only $16 in his pockets and a flatiron in his suitcase, Dedman arrived in Skagway from Portland, Oregon, early in 1898. The panic of 1892 had wiped out his prosperous real estate and bond business, forcing him into bankruptcy. Searching for work in Skagway, Dedman was unable to find any until one of the so-called "soiled doves" entrusted a pair of sheets to him for laundering. He washed them, set them out in the snow to bleach, and returned them to her

Opposite—One of the few houses of the "line" still standing in Skagway is this one located on Alaska Street. During the height of the Klondike gold rush there were numerous houses like this in Skagway. Most of the houses on the "line" consisted of one entry—or living room—and a bedroom.

HOWARD CLIFFORD

cleaner and whiter than they had been for a long, long time.

From then on his laundry business prospered and when his wife Clara and a little daughter arrived in July, he was a partner in the Royal Laundry, a steam-operated plant. Shortly thereafter, George Dedman quit the laundry business and went into the hotel business with a Mr. Hinton as a partner in the Pacific Hotel. Then he entered into partnership with a Mr. Foreman in the original Golden North Hotel, on Fourth Avenue between State and Main streets. Foreman's previous partner had been lost in a dock accident when he slipped from a gangplank.

About 1908 or 1909 Dedman and Foreman purchased the two-story Sylvester Building, which at the time, consisted of retail stores on the lower level and offices on the second floor. It was located at Third and State Street and was converted into a hotel, the present Golden North. As the gold rush waned, so did business, and it was decided to move the hotel more to the "center" of town, where most of the action is.

Skagway did not have the usual house-moving equipment available, much less anything capable of moving a two-story hotel. However, Alaskans had faced problems before, and horses were hitched to a capstan and a long rope to move the building.

Business apparently prospered, because in short order a young carpenter from Montana, Edward Duayne, looking for work in Skagway, was hired to raise the Golden Dome and add a third floor to the structure. (In various records his name also is spelled Dwayne, Duaime and Duame, and his first name sometimes is given as Edmund.)

In the early days, in fact right up until World War II, a great many people from the Yukon—riverboat-

Above right—*The Golden North Hotel pictured in 1908, just after being moved to its present location at Third and Broadway. Later the dome was raised and a third story added by a vacationing carpenter from Montana, Edward Duayne.* Right—*The Golden North Hotel, as it is today.*

men, miners and practically everyone else who could afford it—went Outside with their families during the winter months. A goodly number who got to Skagway by the White Pass & Yukon Route became regular patrons of the Golden North, both on their trips out and on the return, because ship and train schedules did not jibe as they do today. It was not unusual to stop over in Skagway for a couple of days before being able to continue one's journey. Many spent the days and evenings sitting around the old wood stove in the lobby of the Golden North, swapping tales of the gold rush.

Some time in the early twenties Dedman bought out Foreman, mortgaging the hotel to do so. In 1925 George Dedman passed away at the age of 67, and his wife Clara and son Henry continued to operate the hotel until her death in 1936. During the 1920's Mrs.

George and Clara Dedman in front of the Golden North Hotel after it was moved to its present location and a third story added. The Dedmans were early day operators of the hotel. The photo was taken in 1922-23.

DEDMAN'S PHOTO SHOP

Dedman and her son also established a photo business in an old theater building which since has been torn down.

During the 1930's the depression hit Skagway as it did other communities throughout the country. After Mrs. Dedman's death the mortgage on the hotel was foreclosed, and the facility passed out of the Dedman family ownership.

In 1937 James Tropea became the owner and manager of the Golden North, and operated it until after World War II when the Pullen heirs bought the hotel. It was open several years during the 1950's. Once again lack of business closed the doors, and they

RASMUSON LIBRARY, UNIVERSITY OF ALASKA

Opposite—Broadway, Skagway's main street, pictured on May 20, 1898. The Burkhard House, located on Broadway and McKinney. Note the many horses and wagons, some of which probably eventually traveled over the Brackett Wagon Road. Right—This unusual wood-burning stove in the lobby of the Golden North Hotel was the gathering place for visitors during the early days in Skagway. It was used for heat from the time the hotel was built through the 1920's.

DEDMAN'S PHOTO SHOP

remained so until the hotel was purchased in 1961 by Hans and Mavis Soldin and Mrs. Soldin's sister and brother-in-law, Edith and Mark Lee.

The new owners got the word around town that if residents whose families had established themselves in the community during the gold rush would provide furniture of the early days for a room, the room would be dedicated to the family. The response was gratifying and many old-timers turned their ornate and cumbersome furniture over to the hotel, parting with cherished keepsakes, elegant bureaus, four-poster and canopied beds, handsome old mirrors, chairs, marble-topped washstands with bowls and pitchers, and the like. Today these rooms, furnished by old-timers and their families, bear histories and photographs of the gold rushers. Rooms are dedicated to the White Pass & Yukon Route, H. D. Kirmse, the Dedman family, the McCanns, the Dillons, the Richter family, E. J. Liddicoat, Ferdinand De Gruyter, Dr. and Mrs. Peter Crepeau, Mr. and Mrs. Winfield Sparks, Harriet Pullen, the Rapuzzi family, H. D. Clark, Oscar Selmer, Frank Feero, Jim Mulvihill and Edward Duayne.

The hotel was purchased in 1966 by Norm Kneisel of Kneisel Travel, Portland, Oregon, and is used to house visitors traveling through on Kneisel Tours.

After losing the hotel, Henry Dedman went to work as a machinist for the White Pass & Yukon Route. His wife Bessie and their daughter Barbara continued to operate the photo shop, which is now located in the same facility that was used by the famed photographer, E. A. Hegg. Henry Dedman passed away in 1954. Barbara is married to a former soldier, Ed Kalenkosky, who was based in Skagway during the war. They have four children, and the name has been shortened to Kalen.

Opposite—*Holly Street, now Sixth Avenue, in the days of the gold rush. At the right is the Hotel Mondamin, first of the good hotels in Skagway. Three doors down from the Mondamin is the saloon operated by Soapy Smith, taken over by John Clancy following Smith's death. The photo was taken from Broadway, and the post office and bank building are located on the site at the present.*

UNIVERSITY OF WASHINGTON LIBRARY

Above—The Skagway White House was built in the early days by Lee Guthrie, owner and operator of the Board of Trade, one of Skagway's most prosperous gold rush saloons. It is presently one of the community's smaller hotels, operated by Nova and Wanda Warner. Opposite—Fifth Avenue is the street on the left side of the photo. Just below the industrial stack at the right is the Captain Moore home, still in the same location. The Hotel Mondamin is seen just to the left of the stack, at the corner of Sixth and Broadway.

Another of the first-class hotels in Skagway was the Mondamin, on Broadway at Sixth. It was the stopping place for many of the famous persons who visited Skagway during the rush. The hotel register lists such names as John L. Sullivan, Lillian Russell and Lily Langtry. Jefferson Randolph Smith was often a guest, occupying room #61 on each occasion and signing the register Jeff R. Smith. The owners-operators of the hotel were Hansen and Tennant.

The Dewey was the oldest in the city. It was located at 710 State Street, but later was moved down near the train depot. It has since been torn down. In the early days the proprietors were Sloan and Dewey.

Other hotels operating prior to the turn of the century, some of which are long gone and others converted to other uses, included the Brannick operated by E. J. Brannick; the Bay View, H. K. Dent as proprietor; the Butte, V. S. Rider, proprietor; Brogan's managed by Louisa Urban; the Moore managed by Mrs. H. E. Russell; the Astoria with A. H. Davis as the manager; Hotel Wickstrom, Peter Wickstrom, proprietor; Hotel Seattle, A. Birnbaum, proprietor; and the Miners' Hotel, Mrs. A. Crawford, proprietor.

Others included the Occidental Hotel, Ernest Miller, proprietor; Pacific Hotel, C. W. Klippel, manager; Portland Mizpah House, owned by Mr. and Mrs. A. P. Mead; the Ranier with Frank Hall, proprietor; Shoup Avenue House, with H. E. Ayers, proprietor; the St. James, then at Fourth and State, but since moved to Fourth just off of Broadway; the St. Nicholas, with Nicholas Portman, proprietor; the Fifth Avenue operated by Miss L. A. Burke; the Manhattan, managed by George Sexton; the Burkhard, operated by F. F. Clark; the New Home, with the Misses Berkhoffer, proprietors; Travelers Home, managed by Aschwanden & Lumpert; the Magnolia, Charles Carmichael, proprietor; the Grotto, with J. Henry Foster listed as proprietor; and the United States Hotel, W. R. Curley, proprietor.

The Skagway Inn on Broadway is still in operation, and the White House, a former private residence, is another historic building in use today.

THE MONEY LENDER

Whenever and wherever a new community develops, there are those in need of money and Skagway was no exception. Before regular banks are established, and even afterward (for those whose credit might not be up to snuff), money lenders provide this service.

Such was the role of Frank Keelar of New York, California and way points who arrived in Skagway March 9, 1898, from Oakland, California, and established himself and family along with a Japanese servant, in plush quarters in the Hotel Mondamin. He opened offices next door on Holly (Sixth) Street, a few doors from Soapy Smith's saloon, and advertised

Opposite—*Advertisement placed by "Keelar, the Money King of Alaska" in a Skagway publication.*

HOWARD CLIFFORD COLLECTION

himself as "The Money King of Alaska." He declared that he had barrels of money and that no deal was too large for him to handle. He was a dealer in watches, diamonds and jewelry, and claimed that he had iron-covered warehouses for merchandise and baggage taken in as security for loans. He oftentimes referred to the many mines, sawmills, steamboats, packtrains, stage lines, timberlands and townsites that he owned. He called himself Colonel Keelar and stated that he had a steam yacht at his disposal, anchored at Sitka.

Another occasion found Keelar referring to a trip of 45 miles to his "Money Mine No. 7." He made it in 7 hours, he said, with his $3,000 sled-dog team. He claimed to own a sawmill on Big Skookum which turned out 20,000 board feet of lumber a day, for $200 per thousand. Keelar said he had served as a city councilman in a community where he formerly lived, and that he had donated a park to that community and sponsored a boulevard which went from the park to the waterfront. He also revealed that he had been a Grand Exalted Ruler of the Elks Lodge, and that the social affair of the season was held in the Keelar Opera House.

Keelar said he owned a string of 130 pack animals which he kept on the trail, and that he was planning a mammoth icehouse with a capacity of 4,000 tons of clear lake ice for the community.

THE MONEY KING OF ALASKA,

Such were the statements of "The Money King of Alaska," and no one disputed those claims. He later was elected to the Skagway city council and served the community well. Keelar offered a reward of $5,000 to the man "I can't deal with if he wants to trade." His two offices were the showplaces of town. He had a fine collection of the most exquisite old cameos, heirlooms and other jewelry he had swapped useful things for with cold-footed sourdoughs.

In a mail circular sent to those in the States, he further advertised, "If you want to know anything about Skagway, Alaska, and don't want to come and see about it, write to me. If you want to invest some money here or want a partner, DON'T WRITE, as I will not advise anyone to invest, and don't have time to take care of or feed any partners. If you have no money and your skin is full of hard luck stories, don't come to Alaska as we don't have time to bury you. But if you are a man that believes in pluck and not in luck, here is the place of all places on earth to invest, but you must have something to invest."

THE MOLLIE WALSH STORY

There are many women, as well as men, who left their mark on Skagway and the Trail of '98. One such was Mollie Walsh, a dark-haired Irish lass who arrived in Skagway at the tender age of 24 aboard the *SS Quadra* on October 9, 1897.

Although little is known of Mollie's early life, she is believed to have been a dance-hall queen in Butte,

Montana, before heading for the North. She did arrive, however, with sufficient funds to see her through the winter and to establish a grub-tent at Log Cabin the next spring.

Arriving on the same trip with Mollie was the Reverend R. M. Dickey, who took her in tow upon landing and introduced her to the proper families in town. She worked through the winter with the church women, helping establish the community's first church, and then in late March 1898 departed for Log Cabin on the White Pass Trail to set up a grub-tent. Here she fed many a hungry but fundless prospector perhaps the first hot meal he had eaten in many days. She was loved and admired by all.

Mollie had many admirers, but one of her most ardent suitors was Jack Newman, head packer for one of the large trains on the trail. She and Newman parted, however, after he killed a Skagway faro dealer over her affections and followed this with an argument over another admirer, also a packer on the trail.

Newman ordered her not to see the other packer, which was a grave mistake. She married the fellow, Mike Bartlett, who made a fortune at his trade. Later they moved to Dawson City where he was even more successful. Eventually they moved to Seattle and in 1902 he murdered her in a jealous rage over another man.

In the meantime, Newman also married, but always remembered Mollie. A couple of years before his death he erected a monument in her memory which stands at Sixth Avenue just off Broadway in Skagway. "Packer Jack," as he was known, also was responsible for the bronze plaque placed near the summit of White Pass paying tribute to the nearly 3,000 head of horses and mules that were killed on the pass during the gold rush. He also erected a plaque at Sixth and Union in Seattle, honoring his own wife. This plaque is still located there, next to the Washington Athletic Club.

> *Jack Newman was one of the most prosperous of the White Pass Trail packers. Newman was also responsible for a monument erected in memory of the many horses and mules lost on the trail during the gold rush. Packer Jack is pictured here a few years prior to his death in 1931.*
>
> HOWARD CLIFFORD COLLECTION

86

Packers with horses and dogs made their way through the wooded area on the lower reaches of the White Pass Trail in the vicinity of Porcupine Hill. The narrow trail caused huge traffic jams. Hungry horses nibbled hay from the bales being hauled up for fodder.

Early day packtrain at Little Lake on the Skagway (White Pass) Trail. Photo is believed to have been taken in the late summer or early fall of 1897 before improvements were made on the trail.

There were many other prominent packers operating out of Skagway before the White Pass & Yukon Route was constructed. One was John E. Feero who arrived in the North in August 1897. His family, consisting of his wife, twin daughters Ethel and Edith, and two sons, Frank and Bill, joined him on October 19, 1897, when they arrived aboard the steamer *Alki*.

Feero had been in the transfer business in Tacoma, but like so many other rushers, had lost everything in the crash of the early 1890's. He did still have two horses, one of which he gave away prior to heading North, but the other was so ornery he could find no one who wanted it, so he took it with him to Skagway.

Upon arriving he was immediately offered a job by Joe Brooks, one of the established packers, who saw him handle the unruly one and stated, "Anyone who can handle a horse like that can handle any horse." Feero went to work for Brooks at $5 a day and keep.

On his first trip out with experienced packers, the train made 7 miles the first day. The lead packer then staked out the horses with only a handful of grain each and prepared to retire. Feero protested without avail that the horses should receive more feed, and protested even more so when they were forced to resume the trip the next morning with the same bare ration. Feero refused to continue and returned to Skagway where he reported to Brooks. Realizing it was useless to try to get Feero to rejoin the packtrain, Brooks put him to work cooking for the other packers. Feero refused to go out on the trail again unless there was proper food for the horses and a wrangler to take care of them en route. When he did make a trip in charge of a train, it was a most speedy and successful one, without the loss of a horse, which was unheard of in those days.

Joe Brooks and other packers soon learned the wisdom of proper care of horses, which were being bought and sold for as much as $150 each. Feero was also one of the first to use a trained lead pony or horse on the trail. It carried little in the way of a load, but more than proved its worth in leading the train through bad weather on a trail that at times was all but invisible.

Later Feero went into partnership with another packer in the firm of Pells and Feero. He lost his life on the trail during a severe storm in December 1898.

He was within a mile of help at the time, but was unable to make it to a safe refuge. The family remained in the city and eventually, as did virtually everyone, became associated with the White Pass & Yukon Route.

The family watched Skagway grow and decline, and saw the tourists come and go after World Wars I and II. Edith and her sister left Skagway in 1948 and returned to the Tacoma area. John's grandson Bill is still in Skagway, active in business affairs and manager of the Klondike Inn.

Other packers on the Trail of '98 who continued to haul thousands of tons of goods over the summit until the railroad took over included Burton Johnson, the Lewis and Prosser packtrain; Archie Burns and his horse train; Jim Wison and his train of mules; Shorty Kerchner; Charles DeWitt; and Calvin Barkdull to name a few.

Statue of Mollie Walsh, erected by Jack Newman, a former admirer, after she was murdered in 1902 by her husband. Mollie ran a grub-tent on the White Pass Trail and was a friend to all. The statue is located on Sixth Avenue, near Broadway. Bill Feero, Skagway businessman and grandson of one of the early day packers, is pictured with the statue.

HOWARD CLIFFORD

90

Packer Jack Newman's cabin, 1898.

COPY BY VAN NESS

A COLORFUL CHARACTER

One of Skagway's most colorful characters was Martin Itjen, who arrived from Jacksonville, Florida, in 1898, attracted by the discovery of gold in the Klondike.

Martin dug for gold, but never made it to the Klondike. He went over the White Pass, prospected in

Martin Itjen and his famed "Skaguay Street Car." Martin was Alaska's first tour conductor. The "street car" became world famous when he invited Mae West to come up and be his conductor. Martin dabbled in other things also—such as being the town's only undertaker and Ford dealer.

DEDMAN'S PHOTO SHOP

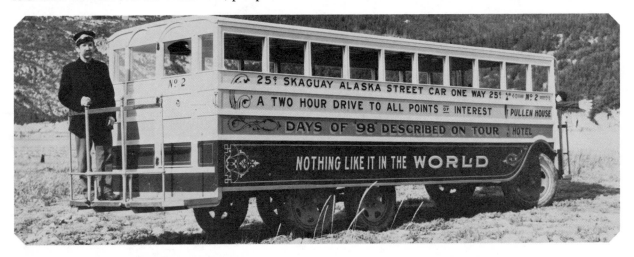

the Atlin area, worked on the telegraph line between Bennett and Dawson City and eventually returned to Skagway where he became a permanent fixture.

During the rush, Martin and his wife Lucille operated the Bay View House, which was built on a barge held above the water on pilings. While prices for everything in Skagway were sky-high, the Itjens charged only 25 cents a night for lodgings, "provided the prospector had his own bedding." A mattress and springs were on each bunk. If the visitor had no bedding of his own, that made no difference. It was supplied by the Itjens at no extra cost. Martin was like that.

At the time they were furnishing their Bay View House, the nearby town of Dyea was being abandoned. The Itjens heard of a sale of furniture and other equipment from one of the Dyea hotels, rowed over and brought back dressers, beds, tables, chairs and other furnishings, a total of five or six loads in as many days. It was not until later that they learned that the man whom they paid for the furniture had no right to sell it. He had just walked into the abandoned hotel and conducted a successful sale for a week or so. Later

Martin went into the undertaking business, but found the town "too healthy" with very little need for his services. He opened the town's first auto sales agency (Ford), operated its first hack, and later founded Alaska's first tourist sightseeing operation, the "Skaguay Street Car Company."

The "Skaguay Street Car" was a bus-like body of a Ford chassis. Martin was a wizard with electricity, and many were the novelties on his various "street cars," four in number. The most picturesque of the cars he constructed was one which carried a stuffed bear cub on the front, the bear growling and pointing to the right or left as the car turned. The bear, Itjen reported, was another creation from the products of Henry Ford. It consisted of one Ford starter, two ring gears, two Bendix drives, two spindle bolts, one horn, one auto wheel, one switch, two headlight bulbs and a few braces, hooks, levers and bolts, all concealed inside the bear hide. It was needless to point out that Martin was the town's Ford dealer, and one proud of his product.

The car also had a little manikin which was operated by foot pedal. He nodded his head, waved a flag and rang a bell with his left foot. The exhaust of the engine came out through a cigarette in his mouth. The next car was larger, as patronage required. Another bear rode on the front and a life-sized effigy of Soapy Smith was on the back, operated electrically. He turned to salute in a military fashion at regular intervals.

Itjen acquired Soapy Smith's place and in 1935 restored it. It became a major stop on his tour of the town. Here, too, he installed another life-sized effigy of Soapy standing at the bar with one foot on the rail, a schooner of beer in his left hand and a gun in his

DEDMAN'S PHOTO SHOP

Right—*A life-sized effigy of Soapy at the bar is part of the present-day Soapy Smith Museum.* Opposite—*George Rapuzzi is pictured with some of the gold rush memorabilia, which he has collected and is displayed in the Soapy Smith Museum.*

DEDMAN'S PHOTO SHOP

94

right. When the front door opened, Soapy raised the schooner in a salute to the incoming visitors and then turned and deliberately shot Dangerous Dan, sitting at a card table in the rear of the parlor.

Itjen added a room to the parlor and used it for displays of other Alaskana. Soapy's since has been moved a second time and enlarged by George Rapuzzi, who obtained it from the Itjen estate.

Martin was long a favorite with the tourists because of his humorous spiel, which kept the sightseers in stitches as he took them about town. His sense of humor and the uniqueness of his "street cars" resulted in his visiting most of the major cities of the United States on a promotion tour for Skagway and his own operations. In Hollywood he gained national publicity by personally inviting Mae West to "come up" and become a hostess on his "street car." Known as the "little man with the big wit," he passed away in Skagway in November 1942.

ONE WOMAN'S FAMILY

The Seattle fire, which a few years previously had destroyed the family operated grocery store, indirectly resulted in the George Rapuzzi family moving to Skagway during the gold rush. The opportunities appeared greater there than trying to recoup and rebuild in Seattle.

George Sr. went North in 1897 and operated a saloon and boarding house on Eighth and Main Street, where the White House now stands. On June 20, 1898, Theresa "Ma" Rapuzzi and her brood of Andrew, Mamie, Charles, Della and Louis arrived on the *City of Seattle* to join her husband. The first family home was a log cabin on Holly Street (now Sixth) and they opened a small business nearby.

The sixth child, George Jr., was born on December 18, 1899. A couple of years later, in 1902, the family moved to Second and Broadway where, with August Garbide, the Rapuzzis founded the Washington Fruit Store. The family lived on the second floor of the store, which soon became the gathering place for Skagway's permanent residents. Home-cooked Italian food, homemade bread and candy from Ma Rapuzzi's kitchen were a favorite attraction. Should any of the regular customers come into the store to make a purchase and find Ma Rapuzzi busy in the kitchen, they made their selection of goods, found their name in the store books, marked down the amount of purchase and left. All paid in full with little or no loss to the store. Ma also made it a policy that no matter how busy she was, she found time to listen to other peoples' troubles and helped them if she could. She always had a piece of candy to give to the little children to ease the pain of an imagined injury.

As the gold rush waned, many people left Skagway but Ma Rapuzzi had faith in the town's future and purchased several of the nearby properties on Broadway, including those housing the present businesses of The Trail Bench, the Shamrock Music Shop, the Red Onion and the Sweet Tooth.

George Sr. died a few years later and the task of raising a family of six fell upon the shoulders of Ma

Theresa "Ma" Rapuzzi and five of her youngsters in front of the family store in Skagway. The picture, taken about 1907, shows, from left in back row, Charles and Andrew; in front are Louis, George, Della and Mrs. Rapuzzi. The family played an active part in the development of Skagway during the gold rush and through ensuing years.

97

Rapuzzi. She did a marvelous job, and continued to operate the store until her death in 1941 at the age of 81 years.

Most of the Rapuzzi family scattered to other points. Mamie married Sidney McDonald and moved to Washington State, where the family operated the McDonald Motor Co. in Seattle's Westlake district. Charles worked as an engineer on the WP&YR until retirement and then moved to Seattle, but he still vacations in Skagway. Louis was a checker on the WP&YR wharf and later was appointed deputy U.S. marshal, serving in this post until he moved to Juneau. Della also worked for the WP&YR until her marriage to J. Aubrey Simmons of the Canadian Customs Service. They moved to Carcross, Yukon Territory, and Simmons served several terms as a member of the Canadian Parliament before retiring and moving to Vancouver, British Columbia.

George Jr. started work as a messenger boy for the White Pass, served as an apprentice in the machine shops, received his papers as a machinist and worked for the railroad until his retirement in 1965. He found time, however, to establish a wood sawing business, garage business, and to secure his captain's license. He operated fishing and tourist trips in the Skagway, Dyea and Haines areas, and for a while had a taxi business.

George gained some local fame in 1923 when he was one of three who climbed the mountain later named Mount Harding, to raise the American flag at the summit on the morning of President Harding's visit to Skagway. In 1926 George met and married Edna Nelson, a Minnesota schoolteacher who came to Skagway to teach. Today she is his partner in various business endeavors in Skagway.

In 1942, following the death of Martin Itjen, the Rapuzzis acquired Soapy Smith's parlor, Martin's collection of Alaskana and his "Skaguay Street Car." George recently restored the vehicle and put it back into operating condition. It is a 1907 Packard and is on display at the museum.

Following George's acquisition of Martin's proper-ties, Jack Gresback, who worked as conductor on the "Skaguay Street Car," operated the museum for the Rapuzzis. At that time it was on Sixth Avenue, but since has been moved to a location near the waterfront. In 1964 George and Edna restored and enlarged the structure and operate it today. ⚞

LANDMARK BUILDINGS CONSTRUCTED

A couple of Skagway buildings which, although built prior to the turn of the century, still attract a lot of attention, are the colorful Arctic Brotherhood Hall, on Broadway near Second Avenue, and the present city hall and Skagway Museum at Seventh and Spring.

The Brotherhood Hall was the home of Camp Skagway No. 1 of the secret fraternal organization founded in the late 1800's, while the city hall was built to be the home of McCabe College.

The Brotherhood was born in the dining salon of the *SS City of Seattle* on February 26, 1899, while the ship was en route from Seattle to Skagway. Eleven men, "as true of heart and as hardy of brawn as ever came together for fun, fight or footrace," got together for the purpose of enjoyment and mutual aid and formed the secret order.

Thomas W. Farmsworth was named Arctic Chief, and as there was no secretary elected, written minutes

of the first meeting are lacking as are records of the first initiation. The initiation fee, however, was $1—the price of a good bottle of beer. Buttons or badges were champagne corks for the officers and beer caps for the brothers not in office.

Upon arrival in Skagway, seven of the original eleven members mushed over White Pass to the Yukon, leaving only Farmsworth and three brothers to carry on the promotion of the organization.

The first meeting in Alaska was held on March 10, 1899, with others considered worthy of the honor being invited to attend. There were 17 on hand for the meeting and the cheechakos were initiated and elected to membership. A more formal organization came about, and the Arctic Brotherhood button, "a gold pan, with the letters A.B. and gold nuggets just below it," was adopted. Meetings continued to be held and the membership grew to more than 300. Some 20,000 feet of lumber, and transportation of it from Vancouver, was donated by members for a meeting hall, and the present building on Broadway was constructed with a value of $5,000. Improvements and embellishments were added in the amount of $3,000 by Charles O. Walker, who applied the 20,000 pieces of rustic decoration.

Other camps were established at Log Cabin, Bennett, Dawson City—eventually about 30 in all. The last member to be initiated into the organization at Skagway was President Warren G. Harding, who became a member when he visited Alaska in 1923.

The Fraternal Order of Eagles Hall, at Sixth and Broadway, is another turn-of-the-century building. It was remodeled and moved to this location from another site. Another early day Skagway fraternal lodge was Skagway Igloo No. 12, Pioneers of Alaska, founded in 1911 and recently reorganized. The Ladies' Auxiliary No. 13 was founded at about the same time, and renewed its activities in 1973.

The McCabe College building came about as a result of the purchase of part of the Moore homesite by James J. Walter on May 31, 1899, acting on behalf of the Methodist-Episcopal Church. That same year the church founded the college in Skagway and constructed Alaska's first granite building to house the school. While the college was under construction, the public school laws in the Territory were passed. They made the enterprise impractical and on June 1, 1901, the facility was sold to the United States government. The building became the U.S. District Court and the 70- by 40-foot second-story room, which had been designed as a chapel and was used as such during 1900-1901, became the courtroom. Today that high-arched room, with the Gothic windows shipped thousands of miles to Skagway, houses the Skagway Museum. The building has also been used as the U.S. marshal's office, U.S. commissioner's office, and once housed the federal jail.

The structure was used for several decades by the district court, but as the population of Skagway declined, there was little need for a federal court and the building was abandoned. In 1956 the facility was purchased by the City of Skagway for a city hall and jail that occupy the first floor. The Trail of '98 Museum, founded in 1961, takes over the second floor.

PEOPLE MUST EAT

Another Klondiker who met with little success in the Yukon but returned to Skagway to become important in the development of the town was Henry D. Clark, who arrived in 1899.

Clark almost immediately formed a partnership with H. E. Nicolai, who like Henry, hailed from southern Wisconsin where both had been farmers. They bought out several squatters and obtained a tract of 40 acres west of Skagway, restored one of the squatter's cabins and proceeded to clear part of the acreage. They were able to raise a spring crop of lettuce, radishes and tomatoes in a greenhouse they erected, and found a ready market in Skagway.

The project proved successful. In 1901 Henry journeyed from Skagway to Tacoma to marry Marion Granger, whom he had known in Wisconsin when she boarded with the Clark family while teaching school. The Clarks returned to Skagway, and the partnership with Nicolai prospered to the point where it was profitable to farm a tract in the Dyea area as well as near Skagway. The Dyea tract, however, was abandoned when the partnership was dissolved 5 years later.

Clark not only supplied the community with cabbage, turnips, beets, carrots, rhubarb and other vegetables, but later added poultry and fresh milk to the market list. He also supplied fresh vegetables to the tourist ships visiting the port, as well as fresh flowers for their tables. The Clarks became extremely active in civic affairs, with Henry serving on the city council and working with the Arctic Brotherhood and Fraternal Order of Eagles. Mrs. Clark was active in the Ladies' Auxiliary and in the Women's Club.

In 1920 the cabin was enlarged, and electricity and a full bath were added. Two daughters were born to the couple. Floris became a schoolteacher, returned to Skagway to teach, married, and then went to Whitehorse and Victoria to live. She became one of Canada's best-known writers, under her married name of McClaren. Dorothy became a nurse, training in Seattle. She married and returned to Skagway where she and her husband went into the hardware business, operating a store at Fourth and Broadway.

After 42 years the Clarks retired from their farm, moved to town and were content to raise flowers and a few vegetables on their city property. Henry passed away in July 1945 at the age of 81 and his wife died early in April 1947, also at the age of 81.

Another early day truck-farmer was George Sexton, formerly a foreman for the government experimental farm at Manhattan and later manager of the Manhattan Hotel in Skagway. Sexton had immediate success with seeds sent him as an experiment by the Secretary of Agriculture. It was his contention that there was no reason why gardens could not be successful in the Skagway area, and he apparently

proved his point. Skagway today has beautiful flower gardens, and many residents grow vegetables. Sexton operated a 10-acre plot near Skagway, growing turnips and potatoes as well as oats, barley and flax.

"It is merely a question of sunshine," Sexton contended. "We have more hours of sunshine here than they have in the East, and consequently, should produce better vegetables. It is not a question of the length of the season, but merely a question of the greatest number of hours of sunshine."

TRANSPORTATION BECOMES A PROBLEM

With Klondike traffic growing heavier by the day, improvements in transportation over the trail set up by Captain Moore became a high priority.

As early as August 1897, traffic on the White Pass Trail was moving at a snail's pace due to the

congestion. At one time some 2,000 adventurers were strung out along the trail, with much of their gear in a sorry condition or practically worthless.

The Chilkoot was still a popular route to the Interior with its various aerial tramways. The Chilkoot Railroad and Transportation Co.'s aerial tramway, Burns' Hoist, the Alaska Railway and Transportation Co.'s bucket tramway and the Dyea-Klondike Transportation Co.'s bucket tram eventually joined under an agreement which gave the Chilkoot an edge. This advantage, however, was more than eliminated by the disastrous slide at Sheep Camp.

In the meantime Capt. Charles E. Peabody, whose Washington & Alaska Steamship Co. owned the *City of Seattle* and other ships, urged George A. Brackett,

former mayor of Minneapolis and an engineer who had helped drive the rails of the Northern Pacific Railroad across the Dakotas, to see if better transportation could be developed over one or another of the passes.

Aboard ship heading North in mid-September 1897, Brackett met J. A. Acklen, a Tennessee lawyer and former congressman. They discussed the transportation question and visited both Dyea and Skagway. Brackett decided that the Chilkoot had the most potential. Acklen learned that a Norman Smith had made a survey over the White Pass and sought him out to join forces in a proposed wagon road from Skagway. An organization meeting was held in Charles Kelley's store in Skagway, with a total of 14 prospective charter members in attendance. Included were David Samson, F. H. Word, H. B. Runnalls, F. H. Clayson, Charles E. Kelley, George E. Bradley, D. McL. Brown, J. H. Acklen, N. B. Smith, V. E. Schwab, John C. Greener, L. K. Hart, George Bullen and Ben Williams.

108

Early day advertisement for the Brackett Wagon Road to Lake Bennett. This was before construction of the White Pass & Yukon Route was started.

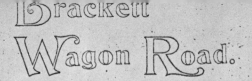

The Brackett
Wagon Road.

SKAGUAY, ALASKA

THE ONLY PRACTICAL WAGON ROAD IN ALASKA. o o o o o o o

Blockades of Traffic Impossible.

A THROUGH SLED ROUTE TO LAKE BENNETT

THE WAGON ROAD AFFORDS AN EASY MEANS OF TRANSPORTATION FOR THE POOR MAN WHO DESIRES TO TAKE HIS OWN OUTFIT TO THE INTERIOR OF ALASKA.

OFFICE:

Third Ave and Main St.

Workmen clearing right-of-way for the Brackett Wagon Road. Work started on the road in the fall of 1897, leading the way to White Pass City. Note how relaxed the workman holding the steel chisel seems to be as the other worker is about to take a swing with a heavy sledge.

NATIONAL ARCHIVES

The group agreed to participate in organizing a company with capital stock of $300,000, of which $150,000 was to go to the charter members for their efforts in time and money.

Acklen and Smith were authorized to return to Washington, D.C., to incorporate. On the way south they again met with Brackett. They convinced him to join them in their efforts, and on October 13, 1897, they incorporated the "Skagway & Yukon Transportation & Improvement Company." C. A. Bullen of the Bullen Bridge Co. was added to the promoters because he owned a 250-foot steel bridge which could be transported to Skagway to span the East Fork of the Skagway River.

Work under the direction of Brackett started on November 8, 1897, with the only money available at the time being $3,500 in Brackett's own personal account—despite the promise of ample funds from the overly ambitious promoters. Brackett had been named superintendent and general manager of the company at $500 a month. As construction started, Brackett learned that the supposed "survey" by Smith was nothing more than hand compass bearings and an outdated Canadian map that had been picked up en route over the trail.

Acklen, who utterly failed to raise funds in the East and was unable to obtain the support from Congress as promised, was soon ousted by the promoters. Treasurer David Samson, too, failed the organization and was removed, and after Smith proved to be useless and unreliable, Brackett was put in charge of the entire operation.

Even without funds, Brackett and his crews completed 4 miles of roadway out of Skagway and opened it to traffic on November 23, 1897. By mid-December, 8 miles had been completed and opened. Bullen's bridge was found to be useless. By December 20, 1897, Brackett was broke. He returned

Opposite—*The Brackett Wagon Road to Lake Bennett, some 3½ miles from the summit of White Pass. Note discarded equipment along the trail. Many Klondikers found the going too rough and discarded their equipment on the spot and returned to the States. Today the White Pass & Yukon Route follows the road for much of the way.*

to Seattle seeking funds from Captain Peabody and others, without success. He went back to Minnesota, and starting with a nest egg from the Great Northern Railroad, was able to raise additional funds from the Canadian Pacific and others.

Brackett returned to Skagway in mid-January and increased his labor force, only to run into trouble in the form of "outlaws" who had taken over part of the trail, claiming they had located minerals under the roadway. A visit by Soapy Smith and some of his followers to the location at the request of Brackett resulted in a hasty retreat of the outlaws and work continued.

Despite the fact that the road had not been completed to the summit and the bridge was not yet over the East Fork, Brackett started charging tolls of 2 cents a pound for freight; $1 for each pedestrian; $1 for each horse, mule, or oxen; 25 cents for each sheep or dog; and $10 for each wagon for use of the completed portions of the road. Hard-boiled freighters and packers refused to pay and destroyed the toll gates erected by Brackett. He wired an old friend in the War Department, who explained to

112

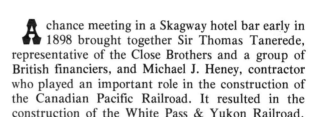

Opposite—*The bridge over the East Fork of the Skagway River was one of the last improvements to be completed on the Brackett Wagon Road. Pictured is one of the first packtrains to cross the newly constructed span. Note toll gate at near end of bridge.*

NATIONAL ARCHIVES

THE WHITE PASS RAILROAD

higher-ups that "a rowdy element had seized the wagon road and had placed the country in a state of terror." That brought assistance from Colonel Anderson and the troops at Dyea.

By mid-April the bridge was completed over the East Fork and the toll road was bringing in a modest $1,000 to $1,500 a day, not as much as Brackett had hoped for. Passage of the amended Lacey Bill, which extended the Homestead Act to Alaska and provided for the construction of wagon roads, trails and railroads, helped but Brackett was still strapped for money and faced a continuing and losing battle with packers and freighters on payment of tolls.

A chance meeting in a Skagway hotel bar early in 1898 brought together Sir Thomas Tanerede, representative of the Close Brothers and a group of British financiers, and Michael J. Heney, contractor who played an important role in the construction of the Canadian Pacific Railroad. It resulted in the construction of the White Pass & Yukon Railroad.

Sir Thomas had come to Skagway with Samuel H. Graves of Chicago and E. C. Hawkins, a Seattle engineer, to finance a railway to the Yukon gold fields if such a project was deemed possible. After taking a look at the terrain, Sir Thomas decided that a railroad could not be built and he had so advised his backers. He thought the mountains too massive and the sheer walls of the cliffs would make the grades too steep.

In the meantime, Heney, better known in construction circles as "Big Mike" (for his accomplishments, not his size) or the "Irish Prince,"

113

had made an independent study of the area and was not deterred in his plan to build a railroad over the pass, provided financing was available. The meeting of the two resulted in a thorough discussion of the terrain and its problems. The talk at the St. James Hotel lasted through the night, and when dawn broke, they drank a toast to the success of the operation.

The White Pass & Yukon Railroad (later known as the White Pass & Yukon Route) was organized in April 1898. Construction began on May 27, 1898, as soon as materials arrived in Skagway.

Previously three Victoria businessmen, who had listened to Captain Moore and his idea of building a railroad over White Pass, became interested in such a project and obtained a charter to build a railroad over the Canadian portion of the route. They were unable to raise the necessary capital, however, and sold their franchise to Close Brothers of London, England, in March 1898.

Close Brothers, although their management had never visited the Alaska Panhandle, prepared to build the railroad provided the proper construction experts could be obtained for the job. They secured a charter of incorporation for the Pacific & Arctic Railway and Navigation Co. from the State of West Virginia, and then obtained the right-of-way to cross the United States territorial land involved.

The London firm had contacted Samuel H. Graves of their Chicago office and named him president of the P&AR&NC. He negotiated with George Brackett, who was building the toll road. An agreement was reached whereby Brackett would receive $50,000 compensation for any damages or losses suffered because of the construction of the railroad. The railroad also took an option to purchase Brackett's "toll road and all its franchises, appurtenances and rights, etc., at any time before July 1, 1899, upon payment of an additional $50,000." Brackett had $185,000 in his project, but realized that it would be impossible for him to build a railroad over the mountains, considering all the governmental red tape of the two nations involved.

Following the purchase of the Brackett right-of-way, the railway engineers surveyed five routes over the summit, but concluded that the best was the one discovered and explored by Capt. William Moore.

Sheer cliffs challenged workers building the *White Pass &
Yukon Route* from Skagway to Whitehorse. No modern-day
equipment was available in the 1898-1900 era when the railroad
was built—only blasting powder, picks and shovels. Pictured is
construction work at Porcupine Hill. Note the two men on the
right using crowbars to pry a boulder over the cliff. Immediately
below is the Brackett Wagon Road and far below in the bottom
of the ravine is the old Moore trail.

UNIVERSITY OF WASHINGTON LIBRARY

In a cost-saving move, the company decided to construct a narrow-gauge line with the rails 3 feet apart, instead of the recently arrived-at standard gauge of 4 feet, 8½ inches. This resulted in a 10-foot roadbed, instead of the normal 15 feet. Following the start of construction, the first passenger train operated a distance of 4 miles out of Skagway on July 21, 1898. By February 18, 1899, the track had reached the summit of White Pass. One of the major obstacles that had to be overcome by Mike Heney was crossing the international boundary into Canada, despite the fact that the money to finance the railroad was British.

At that time the summit of the White Pass was believed to be the boundary between the United States and Canada. When Heney's spike-drivers and track-layers reached the summit they were told in courteous but positive terms that their "wildcat railroad" could go no farther. The Royal North West Mounted Police visited the camp daily and received royal treatment from Heney's crew, but they received instructions from Ottawa that "they shall not pass."

Heney sent his trusted friend and co-worker, "Stikine Bill" Robinson as informal ambassador to the summit, with instructions to proceed in the spirit of diplomacy, and untie the red tape. The story goes that Bill's only baggage on his trip to the summit consisted of a bottle of Scotch in each pocket of his mackinaw, and a box of cigars under each arm.

He found a guard pacing the supposed line. Two days later the guard woke up from a long and heavy sleep, and the first sight he saw was Heney's construction gang working like beavers, laying track well over the international line and already a mile or so down the shore of Summit Lake. After that, construction went ahead without interruption and reached Lake Bennett on July 6, 1899, with the Mounties proving to be helpful cooperators.

117

On July 6, 1899, the first passenger train left Lake Bennett for Skagway on the White Pass & Yukon Route. The train carried more than $500,000 in gold from the Klondike.

UNIVERSITY OF WASHINGTON LIBRARY

Construction started from Whitehorse toward Carcross and the two gangs met at Carcross on July 29, 1900, completing the chain of steel.

Dignitaries of the period, both American and Canadian, took part in the Golden Spike ceremonies. An experienced trackman started the spike upright and gleaming beside the rail. The officials on hand had by this time partaken in the usual Yukon hospitality marking such an auspicious occasion, and despite attempts by all, the spike remained battered but undriven into the tie. Calling it a successful affair the dignitaries retired to continue the celebration.

The track superintendent remained behind, removed the battered spike, replaced it with one less noble and drove it home, thus completing the rail link between Skagway and Whitehorse. Actually the White Pass & Yukon was built and initially operated under three charters, the Pacific & Arctic Railway and Navigation Co. in the United States territory; the British Columbia and Yukon in British Columbia; and the British Yukon Railroad in the Yukon.

The building of the railroad was one of the most difficult ever attempted. The closest base of supplies was 1,000 miles away. Communications between Skagway and Seattle were by letter on coastal steamers which operated on irregular schedules. There was no heavy equipment available and most of the work through the solid rock along the route was by hand drills and blasting powder.

Mike Heney, along with his able assistants, "Stikine Bill," E. C. Hawkins, Dr. F. B. Whiting and others, were later to be involved in the building of the Copper River and Northwestern Railway from Eyak (later named Cordova by Heney) to the rich copper fields of the Interior.

From sea level at Skagway the WP&YR climbs to the summit of White Pass (2,885 feet) in 21 miles. The average grade to the summit is 2.6 percent, with the steepest about 4 percent. The line from terminal to terminal is 110.7 miles, of which 20.4 miles is in Alaska, 42.2 miles in British Columbia and 58.1 miles in the Yukon. Cost of construction was about $10,000,000.

In the early days the rail line was augmented by a river division, with freight and passengers transferring at Whitehorse to the Yukon River sternwheelers for the trip to Dawson City. In the winter the WP&YR operated a stage line with horse-drawn vehicles while the river steamers were frozen in the ice.

There were good years, but by the 1920's gold production had started to fall off and the drop continued through the 1930's. The Yukon's population declined almost to the vanishing point. Some mining operations did continue with silver, lead and zinc production being developed in the Mayo district. The ore was carried to tidewater by the White Pass river and rail divisions and the Yukon communities maintained a reasonable level of business during the summer season, but business dropped to an extremely low level during the winter.

Over the years the WP&YR ran deeper and deeper into the red and at times was barely able to pay its bond interest. In added efforts to keep solvent, the firm went into the wholesale petroleum business long before the invention of tank cars. It also operated an air service, with bush pilots flying prospectors into the distant and rugged areas throughout the North.

Despite all this, during the winter months all senior officers of the company had to work without salary.

DEDMAN'S PHOTO FROM HOWARD CLIFFORD COLLECTION

Above—*Workmen are pictured laying track down Broadway, Skagway's main street, on June 15, 1898. The Occidental Hotel is the large building on the left side. Opposite—"Klondike Kate," one of the locomotives acquired by the WP&YR during World War II, in front of the old depot. The locomotive was built in February 1943 for use in Iran by the Army Corps of Engineers, but converted for use on the White Pass. It was retired in 1960, and sold to Rebel Railroad in 1961.*

DEDMAN'S PHOTO FROM HOWARD CLIFFORD COLLECTION

This was changed dramatically and suddenly by the impact of World War II. Along with the remainder of the Allied world, the White Pass system went to war, and donned the uniform of the U.S. Army. Its rail line and river system were strained to the limits to carry the hundreds of thousands of tons of military equipment and construction machinery which poured over the docks at Skagway and was carried inland to help build the Alaska Highway (Alcan) and the Canol pipeline system.

The Army took over on October 1, 1942, and the soldiers landed in the North Country at the beginning of one of the coldest winters on record. Temperatures dipped to 75 degrees below zero at Whitehorse and stayed under 40 below for weeks at a time. The story of the first winter is a story of hardships, privations and enduring cold that cut sharper than a razor. There were men in the 770th Railway Operating Battalion from the Southern Pacific, Texas Pacific and Sante Fe railroads who had never even seen snow let alone the most frigid weather on the continent. But their unending efforts, hairbreadth escapes and daring rescues pulled them through. On "the toughest

One of the oldest of the White Pass & Yukon Route locomotives is No. 52, on display in Skagway. Purchased in 1898, this Brooks 2-6-0 type originally carried No. 2, but was renumbered following overhaul and modification in 1900. Built in 1881, this locomotive is believed to have seen service on the Utah & Northern prior to being shipped to Skagway. It was retired just prior to World War II in 1940.

HOWARD CLIFFORD

122

Northbound and southbound mixed passenger/container White Pass & Yukon Route trains meet at historic Lake Bennett. It was at this point that the sourdoughs of '98 built their boats and rafts for the trip down the Yukon River to the Klondike gold fields.

WHITE PASS & YUKON ROUTE

hundred and ten miles of track in the world," those GI Casey Joneses never faltered. They piled up a most impressive record.

One time a train was smothered under huge snowdrifts at Fraser Loop, about 30 miles from Skagway, and a snowslide occurred a few miles behind, cutting off all communications in either direction. The engine ran out of water and the crews were forced to draw their fires to keep from burning out the tanks. Coal for the stoves in the passenger cars ran out, and the few aboard chopped up the furniture to keep from freezing in the 30-degree-below temperature. Food soon became exhausted.

After 7 days in this precarious position, the trapped train was finally reached by a tractor pulling three heavy sleds. It had traveled 40 miles from Carcross over the ice of Lake Bennett to reach the spot. The sleds, loaded with food and coal, arrived in time to supply sustenance and warmth before any casualties occurred. Meantime the rotary plows worked from both ends of the snowdrifts, finally broke through and traffic was restored. Lt. Col. William P. Wilson, who had been superintendent of the Burlington's frosty routes across the Rocky Mountains in Colorado, was commanding officer of the battalion.

As spring approached, the battalion received help in the form of five narrow-gauge locomotives which the soldiers called "Gypsy Rose Lees" because they were "stripped for action." The Army purchased additional locomotives from the Colorado narrow-gauge, and freight cars built for service in South America were hurriedly diverted to the North for the WP&YR. This brought about a complete change. Trains were highballed over the pass every few hours. At one time the battalion put 34 trains through the Log Cabin station in a single day. August 1943 was the record month with 45,000 tons hauled, an average of 1,500 tons a day.

The line was returned to civilian management on May 1, 1946, and it looked as if the end was near. The equipment was worn out, business was at a low ebb, and all that remained was old and inefficient. Employees, past their prime as workers, remained on the payrolls long after they should have been retired because there was no retirement plan. The company became unpopular in both Skagway and Whitehorse.

A White Pass & Yukon Route train of today pictured on the edge of Lake Fraser in the Yukon. The WP&YR follows the original Trail of '98 from Skagway to Whitehorse.

WHITE PASS & YUKON ROUTE

Damage claims on shipments ran high. Delayed shipments were blamed on the railroad whether it was responsible or not. The WP&YR became the scapegoat for just about anything and everything that went wrong.

In 1951 a new Canadian company, the White Pass & Yukon Corporation, was formed. The next years were ones of growth and modernization. The White Pass still remains quaint with old-fashioned coaches for the tourist trade, but its locomotives are modern, streamlined diesel units. Even more important, the line became a real pioneer in containerization. It made the big move in the early 1950's. Although not yet booming, the Canadian Northwest at the time was enjoying a period of postwar growth. Mining, prospecting and exploration were on the upswing and had produced a slight increase in the Yukon's annual volume of freight traffic, and with it came the growing awareness of transportation costs and their relationship to the future of the rail line and the territory.

The White Pass entered into containerization with the *Clifford J. Rogers*, the world's first ship designed specifically to handle containerized freight. The

The White Pass & Yukon Route carried military and construction equipment during World War II, to help build the Alcan Highway.

4,000-ton *Rogers* was named after the president and general manager of the railroad for many years.

Rogers came North in 1904 to get his start in the very heart of the Klondike at Dawson City. He worked as an assistant in the freight office, as office boy, ticket agent and at other jobs in Dawson until 1907, before he rose through the ranks to the presidency.

The container ship *Rogers* made more than 500 trips between Vancouver and Skagway in 10 years of service before it gave way to the new WP container ships of advanced design, the *Frank H. Brown* and later the *Klondike*. Both are 6,000-ton vessels, with the *Brown* (named for the president of the White Pass Corporation) launched in April 1965 and the *Klondike* in mid-1965.

In June 1973 Federal Industries Ltd., a Winnipeg-based firm, acquired 50.3 percent interest in the White Pass and Yukon Corp. Ltd., including the shares of the major stockholder, Anglo American Corporation of Canada, Ltd. Federal Industries was formerly Federal Grain, Ltd., owner of Neptune Terminals, Ltd., Vancouver area mineral terminal, which could tie in with the White Pass operation.

MORE RAILROAD WORKERS

The White Pass & Yukon Route played an important part in the lives of other families who came to Skagway. One such family was that of William John Mulvihill, a former railroader who arrived in 1900, too late for the Klondike rush.

"Mull," as he was known, had worked for the Great Northern, Northern Pacific, Soo Line and Canadian Pacific railroads, so he had no difficulty in lining up a job with the WP&YR as a "night trick" telegraph operator at Caribou Crossing (Carcross). When construction on the railroad was completed, Mull moved to Skagway to work in the dispatcher office and was joined by his wife Nellie and three children, Verna, Troy and Harold. Three others were born in Skagway—Vincent, Gertrude and Donald. Mull himself was born in Minnesota in 1873.

Mulvihill became a trainmaster and in 1909 was promoted to chief dispatcher, a position he held until

his retirement in 1942. He was almost immediately recalled from retirement, however, to assist the military in the operation of the railroad during the war. He was prominent in civic affairs, and served as mayor of Skagway for many years. Both he and his wife passed away in 1949 and are buried near the gold rush graveyard, alongside the White Pass tracks at Mull's request.

Mull's son Harold (Mickey) Mulvihill, who had arrived with his mother, brother and sister on May 2, 1901, is one of Skagway's oldest residents in number of years in the town. He, too, worked for the WP&YR, starting in 1917 and retiring in 1965.

Another old-time family in Skagway, but one which was not connected initially with the railroad, was the P. H. Ganty family which moved north from Portland, Oregon, in 1901 when Ganty came to work as a clerk for the old Pacific Steamship Co. A couple of years later Ganty entered into a partnership with a man named Frandson and they operated a grocery and food store. In 1904 Ganty bought out his partner and established the business in an uptown location under the name of P. H. Ganty. Ganty also became the Standard Oil Co. agent for the area and soon acquired the franchise for Evinrude outboard motors. He also did a large export business to the Yukon and British Columbia until the advent of World War I. Ganty was the first to introduce outboard motors to Lake Bennett, and made the first trip between the city of Bennett and Carcross in a boat powered with an outboard.

In 1942 he retired from business and moved to Gig Harbor, Washington, but a year or so later returned to Skagway as the storekeeper for the White Pass & Yukon Route. Included in the job was the maintaining of parts for all the rolling equipment, and for a time the many parts needed for the White Pass & Yukon airplane operation between Skagway and Whitehorse. Ganty again retired in 1944 and moved to Seattle where he and his wife passed away several

129

years ago. There were two children born to the Gantys, a daughter, Marian, who lives in the Southworth, Washington, area; and a son, P. S. Ganty, who operates the Pelican Cold Storage Co., and Coastal Glacier Sea Foods at Hoonah. Until a fire in the summer of 1973 destroyed the facility, he also operated the Sitka Cold Storage Co.

Among Early arrivals were Ferdinand John (Ferdie) De Gruyter, an honest gambler who got to Skagway in March 1898 aboard an old sailing vessel towed up from Seattle. Ferdie was joined by his wife and 13-year-old daughter, Jeannette, on May 22, 1899. They had traveled from Louisville, Kentucky, by rail to Seattle and then on the *City of Seattle* to Skagway.

Ferdie was one of the town's most popular gamblers. He operated a faro table in various saloons and gambling halls in town. It was his wife who so often mentioned that it was "either feast or famine" in the De Gruyter household, depending on how Ferdie's luck ran that day, week or month. On December 10, 1906, daughter Jeannette married A. R. "Tad" Hilliary, who had arrived in Skagway with his mother and four brothers in the summer of 1898. All the

Hilliarys worked at various times and on various jobs with the White Pass.

Tad had served a printing apprenticeship in Dawson City, so he worked in Skagway print shops at one time or another. Having a mechanical bent, he also assisted Bobby Sheldon in working out the correct gears for the car he built in Skagway. The couple gave Ferdie four granddaughters who resided or still reside in Skagway.

Another prominent Skagway gambler was George Dillon, who with his wife (like the De Gruyters) lived high on the hog one week and on pork and beans the next. George in later years was appointed U.S. marshal for the Skagway area. There are many Dillons in the Skagway area today.

Oscar Selmer was Skagway's first barber. He also played the violin at all social functions and conducted the Skagway orchestra. He owned the town's only public bathhouse, where for 50 cents one could wash off the grime and dirt of the trail with genuine hot water and soap. He later served as city clerk for many years and was considered a photographer of note. He raised a big family and today there are many Selmars in the community.

A short-time resident of Skagway during the rush, and one who could be seen doing the rough-tough jobs in town, no matter how disagreeable as long as they were honest, was Jack Holt. He later became a big name in Hollywood, in movie he-man roles.

THERE ARE THOSE WHO NEVER GAVE UP

There were many others who had roles in the history and development of Skagway. Some still remain in the community, or they have relatives who have elected to stay. Some, of course, have moved to regions afar.

One of the real old-timers was the late Mavis Soldin, operator of the Hans Soldin Lumber Company. Mavis, daughter of Mr. and Mrs. David Nathan Hukill, was born in Skagway in 1901, the couple's oldest daughter. The parents came to the community prior to the turn of the century. Two other children, Edith Lee and Duncan Hukill, are present-day Skagway residents.

Hans Soldin came to Skagway in 1924 to work with the WP&YR bridge gang at the summit. Hans and Mavis met in 1926 and were married shortly thereafter. She too worked for the railroad, 5 years as a cook and then 19 more servicing the coaches, a job which since has been taken over by her two daughters. Hans retired from the White Pass as bridge foreman, due to a hearing deficiency. They started the lumber business and also built several apartments in town. In March 1961, Hans and Mavis, along with Mavis' sister Edith Lee and her husband Mark, acquired the Golden North Hotel. The structure, at the time in very poor condition, was refurbished. Mavis and Edith did the painting inside and out. Hans did the carpentry repair and Mark fixed up the heating, electrical circuits and plumbing.

They operated the hotel successfully until 1968 when the partners decided to sell, but not until after they had developed the unique idea of dedicating the rooms to various pioneer families of Skagway. Stories of many of these pioneers are related in this book. The Soldins returned to the lumber business. Hans died of a heart attack in March 1972.

Mavis, who was born in Skagway in 1901, liked to tell of the early days when the town was solid with houses and commercial buildings from the railroad across the river, and from the waterfront to the foothills. Those apparently were the good old days.

By April 1898, when this photo was taken, many permanent buildings were beginning to appear in Skagway. The Astoria Hotel was located at 235 Sixth Avenue and is seen in the photo as is the Kentucky House.

David Hukill, a promoter, came to Skagway with 500 men under contract to work on construction of the White Pass & Yukon Route in 1898. He became ill with pneumonia and the workers went on a wildcat strike for which he was blamed. As a result he no longer worked for the railroad, and in Skagway's later years financial pickings were slim unless one worked for the railroad. Such was the luck of David Hukill.

Following his unfortunate experience, Hukill contracted to cut 500 cords of firewood. He hired the men, his wife cooked for them, and just as the task was completed—before he could deliver the wood—the entire effort went up in smoke when an out-of-control forest fire swept the area. He tried mining without success. His luck always seemed bad.

David Hukill died in 1917, but his widow Catherine was able to keep the family together and feed them despite hard times that followed.

An early railroad builder who remained in Skagway for a good number of years was V. I. Hahn. He arrived in Skagway on May 5, 1898, and was hired as a construction engineer with the duty of establishing the route that the actual rail-laying would take. Hahn ascertained that the grades would not be prohibitive if the track were laid on a circuitous 18-mile route from Skagway to White Pass, with an almost continuous climb of three-and-nine-tenths percent grade to the summit. Hahn became superintendent of the railroad on March 15, 1906, and worked in the same office in Skagway from that day until he retired in 1945. He liked to recall an incident that took place following the slacking off of business after the Klondike gold rush. One of the staff suggested to S. H. Graves, first president and one of the promoters of the line, that perhaps they might get some tourists to come up and help increase revenues. Graves turned to the spokesman and asked caustically, "What in the hell would a tourist want to come to this God-forsaken country for?"

Apparently Graves hadn't reckoned with the American tourist.

The White Pass & Yukon Route administration building in Skagway. This structure has been turned over to the National Park Service as a start of the Klondike Gold Rush Park, an international park proposed by Canada and the United States.

HOWARD CLIFFORD

METROPOLIS OF THE NORTH

By 1899 Skagway had developed into the metropolis of the North. It had become the headquarters for the White Pass & Yukon Route, with company officials, clerks, bookkeepers, division superintendents, operators, construction and section gangs, engineers, trainmen, passenger and freight agents, baggage and warehouse men, all making their home in the community.

The WP&YR shops were capable of building most of the rolling equipment and were well able to handle the rebuilding of locomotives at a great savings over shipping them in and out.

The city itself was "systematically platted, with wide streets, and avenues graded and sidewalked in every direction." The streets and business houses, as well as many of the residences, were illuminated by night with electric lights, both arc and incandescent.

Early day buildings on Broadway in downtown Skagway still in use include some of those shown here. Originally these buildings, from left, housed the Red Onion Saloon, one of Skagway's most notorious houses of pleasure located at Sixth and State Street; the Washington Market, operated by the Rapuzzi family and first located across the street; the Canadian Pacific Railway office; Arctic Brotherhood Lodge No. 1; the Alaska Steamship office; and the Golden North Hotel, located originally near Fourth and State Street.

HOWARD CLIFFORD

There was a fresh-water system "second to none" and the city was "kept clean and is as healthy as attention to sanitary precautions can make it." With an ample supply of water, mains throughout the business thoroughfares, hydrants at street corners and four fire companies composed of some of its best citizens, adequate fire protection was assured, publications of the day reported.

With law and order restored, there was "no more orderly city in the world than Skagway," a Chamber of Commerce report stated. The group was promoting the city as an ideal location to establish a business, with notice that support of the fire department, sanitation, police, street improvements, etc., was by volunteer tax contributions, and the city was "free from debt" and could meet current expenses.

As the gateway to the North, Skagway had become the outfitting center not only for those heading to the Klondike but also to the Porcupine, Atlin and Bennett districts. Yukon sleds were manufactured in town, as were tents, fur robes, sleeping bags, pack bags and ice creepers, plus the "other necessities of those heading to the gold fields."

The Felitz Tent & Awning Co. of Seattle had a branch factory in Skagway. The Frye-Bruhn Packing Co., another Seattle firm, had a packing house at 309 Fifth Avenue, with the slaughter house located on the outskirts of the city. There were prominent law firms such as Church & Day, headed by Walter Church, senior member; and Price & Stevens, headed by J. G. Price.

The Peoples' Furniture Factory was located at Broadway and Eighth, as were the showrooms. E. R. Peoples, head of the firm, was also the town's only funeral director. He manufactured caskets and had the only hearse in Alaska, described as a "beauty."

Another business enterprise that gave Skagway the mark of a modern city was a music publishing house. C. F. Latimer of Latimer Musigraph, which published songs for the *Sunday Examiner*, was manager of the concern. Others involved in the enterprise were the Messrs. Hazeline, Hunter and Lauer, described as "each an artist in his own line, which includes photography, etching, designing and engraving." The house was also able to produce half-tone and line-cut works, with the first product being a map of the Atlin gold region. Among others, two of the early day songs which were published by Latimer Musigraph were titled *The Railway Trail to Atlin* and *Some Mother's Child*.

The Skagway Business College was established by Professor Shorthill. It offered practical courses in stenography and typewriting.

There was a tea importing house, Alaska Importing Tea Co., with J. A. Flinn, manager. H. A. Bauer & Co. Outfitters played a prominent role in the development of the community. Bauer was also one of the early day partners in the Golden North Hotel. The Pioneer Cigar Factory, operated by A. M. Laska, was considered one of the best-equipped operations of its kind in the Northwest.

There were numerous real estate offices, wholesale houses, drugstores, doctors' offices and ladies' apparel shops. Dentists included Constantin Bloch, formerly of Seattle; Dr. L. S. Keller; Dr. Joseph Moudy; and Dr. J. B. Wall.

Skagway Dairy, owned by Henry Shafer, and the Sterilized Milk Co. provided the community with dairy products. There were many "painters and decorators," likewise a goodly number of physicians and surgeons, scores of saloons and almost any other business one could imagine.

AN ATTEMPTED HOLDUP

Frontier towns generally suffered bank holdups, or at least an attempt. Skagway was not to be outdone.

Just before closing time on September 15, 1902, a stranger entered the Skagway Branch of the Canadian Bank of Commerce at 516 Fifth Avenue and demanded $20,000.

Two bank employees were on duty at the time, George Wallace, a veteran of the South African war, and Charles R. W. Pooley. The bank manager, Harry M. Lay, had gone to Whitehorse, and L. M. DeGax, an accountant in the Whitehorse branch, was on the way to Skagway to take over. Wallace was working on the ledger at his desk and Pooley, who was preparing to stow away the cash and gold dust from the teller's cage, had just opened the big safe in the back room.

The stranger had a couple of sticks of dynamite in his left hand and a revolver in his right. He asked Wallace if he knew what he had, and Wallace replied, "Yes, dynamite!"

Wallace acted as if to go to the cashier's cage, but dashed for the back door and yelled to Pooley, "Look out, he's got a gun!"

Just then John G. Price, a prominent Skagway attorney, came through the front door with some $350 in cash in his hand to deposit. His entry startled the holdup man. The robber fired his revolver, either by accident or with the intent of shooting Pooley or Price. He hit the dynamite instead. There was a violent explosion. Flying glass from the front of the building cut Price about the face, temporarily blinding him, and scattering the bills throughout the area. Wallace was blown out the back door and Pooley, protected by the iron door of the safe, was deafened and dazed but otherwise unhurt.

The holdup man died a few hours later at the railroad hospital. It was learned that he had hired a man with a boat to row him to Dyea, to leave at 3:20 p.m. that same afternoon.

The bank was a wreck, and $2,800 in gold dust that had been in the teller's cage was scattered.

Following the explosion, the military used a hose in the remains of the building to wash everything down in an attempt to recover the dust. Four to six inches of the ground around the place was put in barrels and boxes and hauled down to the creek, where sluice boxes were built and the ground "processed" for the gold under the direction of Herman Kirmse. The panning efforts resulted in the recovery of more gold than was believed on hand in the bank at the time. John Price recovered all of his bills, not losing a single dollar.

Temporary repairs were made on the bank, and when it opened the next morning there was a run with many depositors demanding their money immediately. All demands were paid promptly, and later when they tried to re-deposit their funds, DeGax refused to take them, stating that if the customers had withdrawn their funds when they felt the bank was unsafe, they should find some other place to put their money.

After the death of the would-be bank robber, J. J. Rogers, the U.S. commissioner for the District of Skagway, called a coroner's jury composed of Thomas Ray, Theo. Johnson, J. B. Moore, Hugh Caswell and J. Nelson. The jury convened with Dr. S. D. Cameron acting as the examining physician. After hearing the various witnesses and examining the evidence, the jury found that, "The deceased is an unknown man of the age of about 35 years, of unknown nationality & occupation; that the deceased came to his death in Skagway, Alaska, on Monday the 15th day of September, 1902; that in our opinion death was caused by the firing of a pistol, which deceased held in his hand discharged, causing the explosion of dynamite, which he was carrying on his person, while engaged in an attempt to blow up and rob the Canadian Bank of Commerce in the said City of Skagway, Alaska, about 3 o'clock p.m. on said day, resulting in wounds from which he died about an hour later in the railroad hospital in said City of Skagway."

Among the few effects found on the victim's body was a yard of ribbon and a silver dollar.

The robber's remains were taken to a medical clinic for study. Eventually they were placed in a sack and thrown in a woodshed, where they were later discovered by three men including W. T. White, who knew the whole story. The skeleton was cremated, but White kept the skull, which in 1910 he presented to Dr. L. S. Keller. Doc Keller presented the relic to Martin Itjen, who displayed it in his museum until 1926, when the museum was closed.

KERN'S CASTLE

By the early 1900's Skagway had become quite a tourist center. The town was famous for its part in the Klondike gold rush, the White Pass & Yukon Route was popular with visitors from afar, and the cruise ships from California and the Pacific Northwest were making the town a regular stop.

Kern's Castle, formally known as the Scenic Hotel, as it looked during the early days. Located in the Dewey Lakes area, it was Alaska's first tourist hotel. A forest fire destroyed the facility several years after it was built.

Realizing that visitors of the period needed recreation as well as the opportunity to view the scenery and retrace the steps of history, and that hiking, camping, fishing and picnicking were popular, a Skagway jeweler by the name of Peter E. Kern decided to develop Alaska's first and finest summer resort.

On a ledge on Dewey Peaks, some 1,250 feet above Skagway, was beautiful little Lower Dewey Lake and above it at timber line, collected in an old volcanic crater, Upper Dewey Lake, formed by melting ice from Denver Glacier. Between the two was a man-made lake which now serves as the city's reservoir. All were within easy hiking distance from town, and it was in this location that Peter Kern decided to build a three-story log cabin which was formally known as "Scenic Hotel," but which was called Kern's Castle from the very beginning. The trail to the site was so steep that packhorses could not be used for transporting the necessary materials to the location, and everything, including a small boat placed on Upper Dewey Lake for fishing, was backpacked by Indians.

141

Refreshments, meals and overnight accommodations were offered. A Mr. Stamsky was the operator and caretaker of the resort. It was advertised as being in an area where natural beauty exceeded the Tyrol and Switzerland. Tourists were reported as praising the "beautiful surroundings, the virgin air, the foaming falls that cool the atmosphere and soothe the nerves." A tent-camp was set up at the lake, which was renamed Lake Kern but the name failed to catch on.

Kern had come to Skagway from El Paso, Texas, where in 1897 he sold a large quantity of jewelry to a rancher and had to take some 4,000 acres of then virtually worthless land in payment. The transaction broke Kern and he headed for the Klondike, but stopped off in Skagway and opened a small jewelry shop which thrived.

Kern in 1898 published a souvenir tourist guide to Skagway, and it was popular with visitors. He also was president and general manager of the Skagway Scenic Cable Co., and general manager of the Home Tramway Co., neither of which was overly successful.

In 1910 Kern received an offer of $1 million for his Texas land, sold out his jewelry business to Herman

Kirmse and left Skagway, making no attempt to sell the hotel, which had proved to be unprofitable.

In July 1912 a forest fire struck the hillside above Skagway and burned a stretch some 2 miles long and 1,000 feet wide, from the south end of Lower Dewey Lake north to Reid's Falls and about halfway up the hillside toward Upper Dewey Lake. Kern's Castle went up in smoke, along with the surrounding facilities.

Back in the 1920's the site was marked on the Upper Dewey Lake Trail, but since then the area has become completely overgrown and the ruins of the castle obliterated.

Another Memorable Fourth

Just as the Fourth of July parade of 1898 was one of the highlights in the life of Soapy Smith, the celebration and parade of 1905 was one of the highlights in the life of Robert E. (Bobby) Sheldon Jr., who came to Skagway with his father as a 14-year-old youngster during the winter of 1897-98.

That Fourth of July Bobby won first prize in the parade for the most original entry. He entered the first automobile ever built in Alaska, one he had constructed himself, although he had never seen a car prior to building his own. Today that automobile is on display in the University of Alaska Museum at College (Fairbanks).

Dan Cupid was responsible for Sheldon deciding to build the automobile. While working as an engineer in the Northwest Light and Power Co. plant, he was courting one of the most attractive young ladies in town. So was the son of one of the town's most prominent physicians, and he had the use of his father's fancy horse-drawn carriage to go courting. Sheldon had heard about an automobile while passing through Seattle on the way North, and also had seen photos of them in various magazines.

He went to work in secret, although it was necessary to confide in one of the electricians in the plant in order to round up materials for the machine—which to say the least were scarce in Skagway. The engine was an Auto-Marine made in Detroit. It had been salvaged from a small motor launch which sank in Skagway harbor. The wheels were cut down from buggy wheels, with bicycle rims and steam hose with rope inside as tires. A bicycle chain and sprocket served to transmit the power from the engine to the wheels. Steering was a stick handle with a "third arm" of his own invention, a method later adapted by early day auto manufacturers.

Actually, the car was responsible for young Sheldon losing the light of his life. Kindly old ladies advised the young lady not to marry him, on the basis that Bobby was a genius and "that is just one step short of insanity."

Alaska's first automobile with its builder Bobby Sheldon at the control stick. He had never seen an automobile prior to building this one, but later became the operator of one of Alaska's more successful auto stage lines.

DEDMAN'S PHOTO FROM HOWARD CLIFFORD COLLECTION

144

Young Sheldon came to Skagway with his father, who was en route to the Klondike gold fields to join as a partner with Leroy N. "Jack" McQuesten. McQuesten was one of the best-known and best-liked of the traders in the North, and he came out of the Yukon a wealthy man. The elder Sheldon suffered a heart attack on the trail and it was all that the youngster could do to get his seriously ill father back to Skagway and on the way back to the family home in Snohomish, Washington, where he died. There were not enough funds available for Bobby to return with his father.

Young Bobby worked at odd jobs around Skagway. He sold the *Seattle Post-Intelligencer*, ordering 25 copies on every ship coming North. They cost him 5 cents in Seattle, a couple more to ship North, and he sold them for from 50 cents to $1 each in Skagway. One of his steady customers was Soapy Smith, who was most generous in his purchase from young Sheldon, often stopping to pat him on the head and encourage him in his efforts as they chatted man-to-man for a few minutes on a downtown street corner.

Bobby went to work as a deckhand on a small boat in Skagway Bay and later worked in the engine room, gaining mechanical experience which was to do him well in the future.

He became a pile-driver operator and worked on the enlarged and improved wharf constructed by Captain Moore, Skagway's first resident. Later when the military was established at Fort Seward (Chilkoot Barracks), he was selected by Lieutenant Richardson to do the dock work there. He returned to Skagway in 1903 and was an engineer in the power plant until 1908, when he moved to Fairbanks to take over as the power plant engineer for the Northern Commercial Company.

While on vacation in 1913, he received a previously ordered Model T Ford, and during the 2-week period he cleared more than $1,000 hauling miners in and out of town. This led to his forming a stage line from Fairbanks to Valdez after his first trip over the "trail" in August 1913.

One of his early passengers on the Fairbanks-Valdez route, which he operated successfully, was Lowell Thomas Sr. He commented after the ride, "I've just

IN THE LORD'S WORK

paid $100 for the privilege of pushing this car from Fairbanks to Valdez with my baggage on it." It was while in Fairbanks that Sheldon met and married Anne Bergman, who became his wife and lifelong partner.

He was one of the early concessionaires at Mount McKinley National Park, and later became postmaster at Fairbanks, serving from 1933 to 1940. He found time to serve several terms in the legislature, including the first state legislature. Later he moved to Seattle temporarily because of his wife's illness, and on June 3, 1973, celebrated his 90th birthday there.

As a youth working on the White Pass & Yukon Route in the early days, it did not take G. Edgar Gallant long to realize that his life was in the Lord's work. A native of Prince Edward Island, he entered the priesthood, completing his seminary studies at Mt. Angel Seminary in Oregon. On March 30, 1918, he was ordained in Juneau by the Most Reverend Joseph R. Crimont, S.J., the first priest to be ordained in Alaska.

Father Gallant returned to Skagway and served both that community and Haines, and as he related in his own words, "for many years rode the circuit, opening new missions and building churches."

In 1931 he was named superintendent of the St. Pius X Mission in Skagway, and in 1932-33 raised the necessary funds to build and open the school, which accepted its first grade school students in the fall of 1933 with 4 sisters of the Order of St. Ann as teachers for the 40 or so pupils, all boarders. The

school was strictly a mission school, depending on the generosity of the faithful for funds.

In November 1946 fire struck the school and destroyed a big part of the building. With it went all the band instruments used to give music lessons, not only to the students, but also to any interested townspeople. At the time Father Gallant headed the mission, with Skagway-born Rev. H. A. Baker and Reverend Lawrence as directors. There were eight sisters of the Order of St. Ann, and two lay teachers on the staff.

The main building was rebuilt and renewed and four cottages built for housing of the students, with the school becoming fully accredited as a high school. A farm was purchased and a dairy opened which supplied milk not only for the students but also for the

town of Skagway. The dairy, about a half mile from the town, had a new barn, dairy residence, milk house and facilities to pasteurize milk.

The students and staff also raised about 500 chickens, 150 geese, some 50 ducks, and tended a large garden which supplied most of the produce for the school.

The school continued until January 1960, when it was closed due to a lack of a sisters staff. During the lifetime of the school, between 1,000 and 2,000 Alaska Native youngsters received their education there, and the results of the program were excellent.

The Reverend Gallant, who later became Monsignor, was also responsible for tastefully altering and decorating St. Mark's, the first Catholic Church in Skagway, built by the pioneer priests, the Reverend P. H. Turnell, S.J., and the Reverend John B. Rene, S.J. He also built a new chapel and named the edifice after Therese of the Child of Jesus, Patroness of Alaska.

The Reverend Gallant remained in Skagway until 1959, except for 20 months spent in Kodiak organizing the parish there in the mid-1940's. In 1944

The remodeled Pius X Mission and Chapel as it looks today. The building was hit by fire in November 1946, reopened following the blaze and closed in January 1960. The school was founded by Father G. Edgar Gallant.

HOWARD CLIFFORD

he journeyed to Philadelphia to recruit sisters to help with the new hospital at Kodiak. All he needed to do was to mention the need, and he quickly had almost 80 volunteers from the Mother House of the Grey Nuns of the Sacred Heart in Yardley, Pennsylvania. Five sisters were chosen for the Kodiak assignment.

The Right Reverend Monsignor G. Edgar Gallant transferred to Anchorage in 1959 to become pastor of the Holy Family Cathedral. During his career he was vicar-general, first of the Juneau Diocese, then of the Archdiocese of Anchorage. For 9 years he served the Territory of Alaska in the Department of Welfare. He celebrated his last Mass on his 80th birthday, March 17, 1974, and retired to take up residence with the Sisters St. Mary of Oregon at Beaverton.

Skagway also had another facility primarily for Natives of the area. During World War II the military constructed a 150-bed hospital facility about 3 miles from town. As the war activities moved from the Skagway area, in 1944 the Army transferred title to the hospital property to the Office of Indian Affairs, now the Bureau of Indian Affairs. Congress appropriated $200,000 to operate the facility as a TB sanitarium.

In March 1945, it was announced that Dr. (Major) Rudolph Hass, tuberculosis clinician for the U.S. Health Service, would be physician-in-charge of the hospital and the Sisters of St. Ann from Victoria had contracted to furnish nursing service. The hospital opened in April of that year.

The facility was open to both Natives and whites, and during the first few months had 89 patients. Equipped to handle a total of 95, it was staffed by 16 nurses, 1 laboratory technician and 35 other employees. Howard P. Anderson was named administrative assistant to Dr. Hass.

In the spring of 1947, Alaska's first tuberculosis sanitarium closed and the patients, staff and facilities were transferred to Alice Island near Sitka, where the hospital is in operation today in conjunction with the Mount Edgecumbe school.

AN EARLY DAY CONVENTION

Skagway was the site of one of the first conventions that eventually led to the establishment of the Territory and later statehood. The stampede to the Klondike had brought attention to Alaska and it was the demands of gold seekers for law and order that brought Congress to consider the needs of the neglected land.

The 55th and 56th Congresses between 1897 and 1901 devoted considerable time to Alaska's problems. There was much disagreement as to the type of government needed. Some favored an appointive legislative council, others Territorial government, and the War Department favored a form of semi-military rule.

Solutions began to appear. The Transportation and Homestead Acts of 1898 freed the railroads from the Interstate Commerce Commission, and provided for homesteading of the land. Next was the Criminal Code of 1899. This provided for law enforcement but showed the need for some source of revenue for the "district."

Liquor was still outlawed, although it was sold freely throughout the area. Governor John G. Brady argued for its legalization under high license but was strongly opposed by missionaries and the Federation of National Temperance. Congress, however, not only agreed with the governor but also extended the tax to fisheries, gold mines and railroads. Railroads paid $100 for each mile of track, canneries 4 cents a can for salmon and 10 cents on each barrel of salted fish, with comparable levies on gold mines. Funds thus derived were deposited in the Alaska Fund payable to the United States Treasury and were to be used to enforce the new criminal code and other uses which from time to time were deemed essential.

The Carter Bill, which divided Alaska into three judicial districts, provided for the moving of the capital from Sitka to Juneau, for incorporation of the more populous towns, establishment of municipal schools and a historical library and museum in the new capital.

Automobiles replace horses and wagons—and there are fewer people on the street—but downtown Skagway looks little different today than it did during the gold rush. This is Broadway, the town's main street, looking northeast from the waterfront. Richter's store, one of several early day businesses still prospering, is on the right.

WESTERN AIRLINES

Legislation passed between 1897 and 1901 gave Alaska some additional machinery for a civilized existence. Although the results were far from satisfactory to many Alaskans who had hoped for an elected delegate and Territorial legislature, the legislation at least helped them set their affairs in some kind of order.

These measures of reform came just in time. By the late 1890's public opinion in Southeastern Alaska was aroused by what was considered federal neglect. Juneau and Skagway showed strong resentment of existing conditions. Public meetings were held. Discontent reached a peak in the summer of 1899.

On an invitation from the Skagway Chamber of Commerce, delegates from Ketchikan, Douglas, Juneau, Sitka and other Alaska centers assembled in Skagway. The convention drew up a memorial asking for many needed reforms (all of which were established by the Carter Act of 1900) plus the right to send a delegate to Congress.

The committee sent a representative, John C. Price, to Washington, D.C., because they supposed the passing of the Carter Act was imminent, but Price failed to impress the federal lawmakers of the need for a Territorial or district delegate to Congress. At the Skagway Convention many delegates favored requesting Territorial government. There was no doubt, however, that a straw vote of the people of Alaska would have resulted in a negative vote for such action. Few people outside of Southeastern Alaska favored it, and the people of the Southeast wanted it only for their own section.

Communications between the Panhandle, the Bering Sea and the upper Yukon regions were so limited that any centralized Territorial government would have been faced with almost insurmountable difficulties. Still there was overwhelming weight of public opinion favoring Alaskan representation in Congress, even though settlements in the Interior could not conceive how an election might be managed.

On May 7, 1906, the 59th Congress passed the Alaska Delegate Bill giving the Territory the right to elect one delegate to Congress. He would not have the right to vote but would serve as an information center for things Alaskan. Thomas Cale, a miner originally from Wisconsin, was elected to the 60th Congress and

Frank Waskey, a young prospector from Virginia, to the short term left in the 59th Congress.

Territorial status came on August 24, 1912, and the first Territorial legislature assembled in Juneau March 3, 1913. Alaska became the 49th state on January 3, 1959.

AND TEMPERANCE ARRIVES

The Territorial legislature passed a resolution in 1915 calling for a vote on a bill entitled, "An Act providing for an expression by the people of the Territory of Alaska as to whether or not intoxicating liquors shall be manufactured or sold in the Territory of Alaska after the first of January 1918."

The resolution was on the ballot for the general election of November 7, 1916, and to the great surprise of many, prohibition was voted by an overwhelming 9,052 "dry" votes to 4,815 "wet" votes, despite a majority of the communities having voted wet in local option elections just the preceding year.

Because there was some doubt as to how far the Alaska legislature could go in regulating liquor, Congress responded to the expression of the will of the people on February 14, 1917, with "An Act to prohibit the manufacture or sale of alcoholic liquors in the Territory of Alaska." This became known as the "Alaska Bone Dry Law" which became effective on January 1, 1918, more than a year before national prohibition.

Liquor first came to Alaska with the Russians, the first reference to alcoholic beverages being in 1741. Both the Russians and the Hudson's Bay Company, however, recognized the danger inherent in the liquor traffic among the Natives and on May 13, 1842, signed an agreement to suppress it.

With the purchase of Alaska, the Territory was placed under the jurisdiction of the Army and classified as "Indian Country," which automatically excluded liquor. Later, on July 27, 1868, Congress passed the Customs Act which among other things prohibited the sale, importation and use of distilled liquors. For some 30 years the Army, Navy, Marines, Revenue Service, Customs Service and the U.S.

marshals and their deputies tried to suppress liquor with notable lack of success.

It was under such "arrangements" that the Klondikers hit Skagway, Dyea and other ports. At the height of the rush Skagway had some 60 saloons and liquor-dispensing agencies, plus three breweries: The Skagway Brewing Company, capable of producing upward of 30,000 barrels a year, owned by W. F. Matlock and R. C. Smith with Herman Barthel as brewmaster; the Skagway City Brewery, owned and operated by Charles Saake; and the Gambrinus Brewery, owned and operated by Fritz Gamsnider. All advertised their products despite it being strictly illegal. Nothing was done to put a stop to the manufacture or sale of alcoholic beverages.

The battle against liquor started in Skagway in 1900 when the first Woman's Christian Temperance Union was formed by Mrs. S. E. Shorthill, who came to Skagway in 1897. Mrs. Shorthill immediately became active in all efforts for the promotion of moral enterprises. The erection of a building to serve as church and school was secured largely through her activities. In 1899 Mrs. Shorthill was appointed representative in Alaska of the National W.C.T.U., and for 6 years she spread the gospel of prohibition in that part of the Territory. Other unions followed, and temperance speakers included Alaska on their itineraries.

Not all the liquor in Alaska was manufactured in approved breweries or was imported from the States or Canada. The Indians of Southeast Alaska were proficient in the manufacture, in crude stills, of a fiery product from a molasses base. The development of such a process reputedly took place at Kootznahoo Inlet, Admiralty Island, and the product became known as "hoochinoo." This in time was shortened to "hootch." It seems to be the only purely Alaskan term that has entered the American vernacular.

It was impossible to enforce prohibition without funds and governors of Alaska and other officials had continually petitioned the President and the Congress to repeal the prohibition law.

In 1899 the 55th Congress, by what was termed "extraordinary parliamentary legerdemain," repealed Alaska's prohibition laws. It was not easy. In the House, 172 members did not vote at all, 13 answered "present" and the repeal carried by a margin of 94-75. In the Senate the vote was 40-11, with 30 not voting.

Prohibition was replaced by a local option, high license fee system. Licensing was done by the judges of the U.S. district courts (there were three at the time, but later four) with an applicant for a license required to show a majority of the white men and women over the age of 21 and living within a 2-mile radius of the proposed saloon approved the granting of the license. Annual fees for saloons were $500, $1,000 and $1,500, depending upon the size of the town.

The distribution of the revenues from these fees played an interesting role in the various communities. In incorporated towns, the revenues went to the town council. Fifty percent of the total was for the support of schools, the remainder for general municipal government. In some towns the liquor fee was the entire tax load. License fees collected outside of incorporated towns went to a special Alaska Fund in the U.S. Treasury with disbursement being 65 percent for use in building roads and trails, and 25 percent for support of schools. The remainder was for public welfare and district courts.

Towns became indebted to liquor license fees. Construction of schools, streets and the like was budgeted on expected income. Skagway just prior to prohibition had spent several thousand dollars on sidewalks, expecting forthcoming saloon license fees to cover the costs. Other towns were in parallel predicaments. It was not surprising that local option elections, with the rare exception of Sitka and one or two other communities, always went heavy to the wet side.

It was under such conditions that the first Territorial Convention of the Woman's Christian Temperance Union was held May 13-16, 1915, in the Methodist-Episcopal Church. Mrs. L. A. Harrison, daughter of the early day leader, Mrs. Shorthill, was treasurer of the Skagway chapter. Mr. Shorthill had become influential and was secretary to the governor of Alaska. Mrs. L. H. Pedersen, formerly of Douglas, but a Skagway resident by this time, was treasurer of the Territorial union.

The program, which attracted 14 voting delegates and other followers from throughout the Territory, was led off with a parade of schoolchildren carrying

Old buildings on Broadway, at the corner of Third include, from left: The Mascot Saloon, Admiral Steamship Ticket office, another office building, the old Salvation Army building (moved here from another location), and a gunsmith and express office. Most of these buildings were unoccupied at the time this photo was taken in 1973.

HOWARD CLIFFORD

flags and banners through the town. The highlight of this Territorial Convention was the appearance of Mrs. Cornelia Templeton Hatcher, president of the Alaska branch of the W.C.T.U. Mrs. Hatcher had come to Alaska as a member of the National Editorial Association in 1908. She was then managing editor of *The Union Signal*, official organ of the national W.C.T.U., and president of the Illinois Women's Press Association.

She returned to Alaska in 1910 on a lecture itinerary for the national W.C.T.U. and spent 4 months in Seward as the guest of Mrs. Pedersen. In March 1911, Mrs. Hatcher, then Mrs. Jewett, was married to Robert Lee Hatcher, a sourdough who came to Alaska in 1896 and was the oldest prospector in the point of service in the Willow Creek section, where he blazed many trails and located four properties, notably the Alaska Gold Quartz Co.'s mine, the best producer in the district.

Following the elections of 1916, Alaska remained dry until the repeal of the Eighteenth Amendment by the Congress and approval by the necessary 36 states on December 5, 1933.

SKAGWAY COMES A LONG WAY

Prior to the turn of the century Skagway had become the largest city in Alaska, with a population estimated at about 15,000.

This was despite the fact that less than a year previously Skagway was the subject of international controversy. Both Canada and the United States claimed it as their own. The Canadian government maintained a customs officer in the town and although Canadian officials moved to the summit of the White Pass in September 1898, it was not until 5 years later that the international boundary was finally established by the Alaska Boundary Tribunal.

The dispute came about as a result of the Treaty of 1824 which the United States claimed gave the heads of all ocean inlets to the United States, including Lynn Canal and Skagway, even though they were farther from the open sea than the treaty allowed.

Cargo ships load day and night in Skagway's small but busy port.

The Canadians rightfully claimed that the Klondike was on British soil and that all would-be prospectors should buy their supplies in Canada. As a result, a stiff import duty was demanded of all American argonauts as they crossed into Canada. The Americans replied by requiring duty on all Canadian goods crossing the Panhandle, or that they be transported under U.S. guard "in bond." The guards were paid at the rate of $10 a day, and thus every man paid tribute to one government or the other.

Despite such disputes, in 1900 Skagway became Alaska's first incorporated city—although this is disputed by some. Skagway and Juneau were both in the running. Skagway held its election a day ahead of Juneau, but waited several days for the elected councilmen to meet and organize. Juneau's elected officials met and organized the day after the election, and thus became the first functioning government under the act of June 6, 1900.

As the Klondike rush subsided, bringing about the decline of Dawson City and in turn Skagway, prospectors turned to other areas, such as the golden beaches of Nome. By 1910 Skagway's population had dwindled to 600 persons, and the town settled down to being the port city for Yukon Territory. The White Pass & Yukon Route and a few tourists provided it with its only income.

After World War I the large cruise ships steamed up the Lynn Canal to Skagway to visit this famous town. Enterprising businessmen stayed to make money from this new rush.

World War II woke Alaska from its slumbers with a start. The Alcan Highway (Alaska Highway) was pushed through; pipelines from Haines and Skagway fed badly needed oil and fuel to the Interior; the WP&YR was improved and the population swelled to some 2,500 persons. In addition, thousands of military personnel trod its board sidewalks and unpaved streets. As before, they left when the boom was over and once again the town settled down to 600 or so permanent residents.

Today Skagway is a small but busy port. It is still the shortest and most direct route to the heart of the Yukon. Silver, lead and zinc ore, and long-fiber asbestos, have replaced gold as the most important cargo coming out of the Yukon.

161

The WP&YR is involved in a multi-million-dollar building program, improving the roadbed and adding much rolling stock to handle the large tonnage of base metals from the new mines in the Yukon. Large containers are loaded with lead and zinc concentrates from the Anvil mines and shipped through the new bulk ore terminal which now dominates Skagway's harbor, bound for smelters in Japan and West Germany. Anvil shipped nearly half a million tons in 1971, and other Yukon mines had smaller but comparable tonnages. Large amounts of asbestos and some copper are also being sent south. They are loaded at the old WP&YR dock, originally constructed by wily Capt. William Moore.

In Skagway proper, the atmosphere is definitely Gay Nineties. Business people and the town's citizens make an effort to hang onto as many relics of the gold rush history as possible. Wooden sidewalks remaining in some parts of the downtown area are a hard-won triumph for the history-minded over the progress-directed. The old false-front buildings are genuine but far-too-few reminders of a hastily erected frontier town.

The Eagles Lodge stages a "Days of '98" show every night there is a cruise ship in port during the summer months, featuring gambling for phony money, kangaroo court, floor show and can-can dancers, and the dramatization of Robert Service's *The Shooting of Dan McGrew.*

The need for equipment for the town hockey team back in 1923 resulted in the idea for the Days of '98 show.

The White Pass had constructed a fine arena for the local skaters, with a gymnasium, dance floor, reading rooms, billiard room and other facilities including baths and showers, which many homes of the day did not have. The arena was open around the clock and proved to be a popular gathering place.

The Skagway team challenged Whitehorse, but found equipment lacking, hence the start of the Days of '98 show to raise funds. Over the years the show has been sponsored by both the Eagles and the Chamber of Commerce. Equipment came from some of the early day gambling halls.

On February 23, 1923, the two hockey teams played their first game, with Skagway winning 5 to 3 on the

frozen Yukon River behind the White Pass shops in Whitehorse. The series continued for many years, with the arena located where the Klondike Hotel stands today being used until 1938, when demolition of the building was started. The war, however, saw the military take over the shell of the structure for a warehouse.

Skagway and Whitehorse have remained friendly rivals and have exchanged athletic and cultural programs over the years, with the railroad bringing the two closer together. For Skagway, Whitehorse is practically a sister city and until recent years the town remained on Yukon time rather than Pacific Standard.

163

A NATIONAL PARK?

As early as 1933 the idea of a national park or monument for Skagway and the surrounding area, including Dyea and the Chilkoot Trail, was being considered. The Skagway Chamber of Commerce in July 1934 named a three-man committee of prominent residents composed of E. A. Rasmuson, W. C. Blanchard and Father Edgar Gallant to push a proposed national monument.

Rasmuson had come to Skagway as a U.S. commissioner after serving as a Swedish Convenant missionary at Yakutat, later becoming an attorney in Minneapolis and returning to Alaska to practice law in Juneau. Upon the founding of the Bank of Alaska he was appointed corporate secretary, and in 1917 was named president. The bank had branches in Anchorage, Skagway and Wrangell.

Rasmuson retired as president to become chairman of the board, and was succeeded by his son Elmer E. Rasmuson in 1943. The senior Rasmuson died in Minneapolis in 1949. Elmer was born in Yakutat and his sister Evangeline (now Mrs. Robert Atwood of Anchorage) was born in Sitka. They moved to Skagway with their parents. The younger Rasmuson followed his father's footsteps in being named chairman of the board of the National Bank of Alaska, and also served as mayor of Anchorage. He has been active in financial, civic and fraternal as well as political activities throughout the state.

After considerable study and discussion between the Skagway committee and the Department of the Interior, a proposal was made that possibly Glacier Bay National Monument could be enlarged to include the Skagway proposal. Chief George M. Wright, detailed to make a study of the proposals, recommended against the development on the basis that two inholdings—Skagway and the right-of-way of the White Pass & Yukon Route—would constitute undesirable encroachments, and that the proximity to Glacier Bay National Monument militated against its incorporation into the national park system. This resulted in the program being pigeonholed until 1961

when, following admission of Alaska to the Union as a state 2 years previously, the program was revised to its present form.

The National Park Service is at present in the process of trying to establish a "Gold Rush Historical Park" which will take in part of downtown Skagway, the remains of Dyea, the old Chilkoot Trail to the summit and from White Pass City to the summit of White Pass. The WP&YR recently deeded its historic old wooden depot in Skagway to the Park Service.

Several years ago the State of Alaska started construction on the highway between Skagway and the British Columbia border and completed 3 miles of the route before work was discontinued due to the fact that nothing was being done on the Canadian end.

In 1973 the Canadian government announced plans to complete the Carcross-Skagway highway, with the construction of the 33.6 miles of roadway to the Alaska border to be completed within 3 years at a cost of $10 million. The road will give Canada access to a deepwater, ice-free port and also will provide impetus to the growing Yukon tourist industry. At the same time the State of Alaska let a contract and agreed to resume work on the remaining 14 miles of highway to the border, with an anticipated 1975 completion date.

Thus Skagway is still the home of the North Wind, but is also one of the friendliest towns in all of Alaska. Once again it is to become a gateway to the riches of the Northwest and the Yukon.

The Pack Train Inn in
the foreground and
the Golden North Hotel in the
right background are two
reminders of the 1898
Klondike gold rush. Both
are as popular with
present-day visitors to
Skagway as they were in
the early days.

ALASKA TRAVEL DIVISION

166

BIBLIOGRAPHY

NEWSPAPERS (Various dates), PUBLICATIONS

Daily Alaskan (Skagway)
Fairbanks Daily News-Miner
Juneau Empire
The North Wind (Skagway)
Rocky Mountain News (Denver)
Seattle Post-Intelligencer
Seattle Times
Skagway News

Alaska Blue Book Tour Guide, Western Airlines, Seattle, 1973.
The Chilkoot Trail, Guide to the Gold Rush Trail of '98, State of Alaska, Department of Resources, 1972.
Klondike Gold Rush Park Master Plan, National Park Service, 1971.
Okuruk, Calgary, Alberta, June 1973.
Pathfinder, Valdez, Alaska, various dates.
The Steel Went North, A Brief History of the White Pass & Yukon Route, Roy Minter, Ottawa, Ontario, 1964.
Souvenir of Skagway, P. E. Kern, Skagway, Alaska, 1908.
White Pass Container Route News, Whitehorse, Y.T., various dates, 1970-1974.
The Voice of Alaska, Sister Mary Joseph Calasactius, Sisters of St. Ann Press, Lachine, Quebec, 1935.

OTHER MATERIALS

Dedications in the Golden North Hotel, Skagway, Alaska.
Harriet Pullen, papers and booklets from Mary Kopanski.
Herman Kirmse, papers and reports from Mr. and Mrs. Jack Kirmse.
Papers and books from Sister Mary Luca, Sister Superior, Sisters of St. Ann.
Papers and letters from P. S. Ganty, the Right Reverend Edgar Gallant and Jack Conway.
Papers and pamphlets in the Northwest Collection, University of Washington Library, Seattle, Washington.
Soapy Smith, papers and letters from Joseph J. Smith.
W. C. (Skagway Bill), Fonda Notebooks, University of Washington Library, Seattle, Washington.

INTERVIEWS

Cy Coyne, Jack and Georgette Kirmse, Mary Kopanski, Edna Rapuzzi, Frances Richter, Bobby Sheldon, Mavis Soldin, Joseph J. Smith and Randolph J. Smith.

SPECIAL RESEARCH ASSISTANCE

Joseph J. Smith, grandson of Soapy Smith.
R. N. De Armond, editor of *The ALASKA JOURNAL.*
Robert D. Monroe, Head of Special Collections, University of Washington Library, Seattle.
Paul McCarthy, Archivist-Curator of Manuscripts, University of Alaska, College.